Overcoming Addictions

Overcoming Addictions

We All Have Them

CB Warsteane

To order additional copies of this book, contact:
Xlibris Corporation
1-888-795-4274
www.Xlibris.com
Orders@Xlibris.com
95969

Contents

Preface

There is no doubt that addiction, as it relates to illegal drug use, is interwoven into the crime and violence fabric of our society. Nor is there any problem the solution to which is more important to the general welfare of our nation.

While the focus of this book will be on how to deal with the illegal classification of addiction, yet it goes further.

The emphasis, from the outset, is on the addiction to illegal drugs; however this is not the complete picture. It is merely the main ingredient in the total mixture of addictions in general.

Whether benign or harmful, legal or illegal, all addictions are subject to the same dynamic universal forces of change and development.

It is the lack of understanding of these "forces" of change, the author believes, which has militated against a higher successful rate of rehabilitation among those seeking to rid themselves of their addictions.

Gaining this understanding, together with a knowledge of the role of the subconscious mind as it relates to all habits, will enable hundreds of thousands of individuals to free themselves from their addictions.

Within this book, for those who make the decision, is a road map that assures a successful journey to recovery.

As a result there is no doubt in my mind that the demand for drugs in general and illegal drugs in particular will be dramatically reduced.

This reduced demand will, in turn, have a significant positive consequence for our entire social order.

For, in the final analysis, it is not the supply but the demand that must be effectively diminished if the struggle against the onslaught of drugs upon our nation is to be successful.

CB Warsteane, J.D.

Introduction

Basically this book is about change and, more importantly, how it takes place. This is so because recovery from addiction, of necessity, involves change.

This is not only because there must be an alteration of our lifestyles if we are to successfully rehabilitate ourselves, but also because we must grasp a method by means of which to accomplish this desired change.

Our nation's most noted scientist, Dr. Albert Einstein, demonstrated, unequivocally, that change is a universal reality. This he did by showing the continuous movement within the atom. Since this is the smallest particle of matter, the logical inference was that all objective forms of things and processes are in continuous movement; always coming into existence, developing, declining and ultimately passing away. This movement pervades the entire universe. It is ubiquitous. It is omnipresent. Only change itself is absolutely without change! It is the only constant that occurs throughout the universe!

The practical application of this fact to addiction provided the basis for an entirely different approach to overcoming addictions. The misguided notion of "once an addict, always an addict" was thoroughly discredited. However, that this movement is basically gradual, unnoticeable, evolutionary and quantitative in its form does not exhaust the matter. Indeed, there is another important aspect of change which is distinct from the smooth, slow and imperceptible changes. There are sudden appearances of things that did not exist before, something new. Furthermore, the change that is in the process of becoming is often the opposite of what previously existed. Thus positive can become negative, new becomes old, and even truth can become untruth (with different circumstances). Therefore, as opposed to the traditional method of analysis, things and processes can no longer be permanently fixed and in separate, unchanging categories. No longer is it either this or that. Now it can be, and often is, *this* at the same time it is becoming *that*! Therefore, the two forms of existence can exist simultaneously! The practical application of this fact to addiction validated the view that anyone can become addicted and anyone can recover. Understanding and applying the correct method is truly the key! The choice, then, is ours to go either way.

However, we must see things as they are and not as they appear to be. Equally important, if not more so, we must see them as they are becoming something else! Seeing them as they are and as they are becoming means interrelated with, interdependent upon, and inseparable from their surrounding circumstances. For phenomena do not exist in a vacuum and it is futile to completely understand any process or thing without taking into account the external circumstances. As well as its internal nature.

Finally, but by no means of lesser importance, we must understand that the subconscious mind is the seat of all our habits and addictions; that it is our spiritual link to the universal force governing the process of change and is spiritual in nature.

For any addiction to be changed into a non addiction form of existence, it is necessary and vital that the subconscious mind be positively reprogrammed.

Attempting to overcome any addiction by eliminating this process is a futile and impossible task. Understanding this fact as well as how universal change takes place are the noble ends to which this book was written.

CB Warsteane, J.D.

Addiction & Habit

When we think of addiction it is usually viewed in terms of the drug addict or the alcoholic. It is not common to include those addicted from the use of prescription drugs.

However, the fact of the matter is that, in one way or another, we all have addictions. Regardless of to what or to whom we may be addicted, the method to successfully overcome is the same.

At the outset we must have a clear understanding of just what addiction is. Loosely speaking addictions are habits. However, all habits are not generally considered to be addictions so let's undertake to define them.

An addiction, according to Webster, is "to make dependent on something such as a drug, etc. to be psychologically or physically dependent". Habit is defined as "custom, especially one hard to depart from and one's usual behavior".

Whether habit or addiction, the successful treatment programs use a definition that dissolves the distinction. To them the decisive factor is, does behavior exist which is "excessive"?

Since we are concerned with treatment and the ultimate change from addiction to recovery, we shall not only consider it as excessive behavior, but will also make another classification. It will be considered either as harmful or harmless; negative or positive; detrimental or beneficial. Again the key is whether or not the behavior is excessive, for it is only then that problems begin to surface; otherwise harmless or positive habits present no problem.

For example: A doting mother's "usual" and "customary behavior" may be that of giving in to the whims of her child.

Again, one's "usual" and "customary practice" may be to have one or two cups of coffee every morning. This is no doubt harmless and beneficial in terms of mentally and emotionally preparing one for the daily schedule. However to drink coffee interminably during the day is "excessive behavior" and could be harmful and detrimental to the body.

We see, therefore, that habitual excessive behavior is at once addictive and such addiction can be either positive and harmless on the one hand or negative and harmful on the other. In other words we may have bad habits or good habits, however, when they involve "excessive" behavior they are invariably detrimental for then they become a higher stage of habit, namely addiction.

Addictions have an even further significant classification. They can be either legal or illegal. Cigarettes and alcohol, used excessively have more harmful and detrimental effects than marijuana or cocaine but their consumption is not illegal per se. One can be addicted to, and therefore have the habit of, consuming "excessive" amounts of nicotine and alcohol (both now established drugs) and as long as such consumption remains within, say the confines of his home, no law has been broken. Obviously this is not the case with drugs such as marijuana and cocaine.

Since successfully overcoming any addiction involves change from a lesser to a more desirable state of behavior, it behooves us to understand just how change takes place. Thus we must fully understand the universal laws of change and development. It is these laws that gave rise to our addictions in the first place and it is these laws which determine their course of development. By having a thorough knowledge of how they operate we will be able to consciously and effectively influence the direction and path we desire the change to take in our lives. We will thereby be able to defeat our addictions and successfully recover.

Change & You

As you view yourself in the mirror there are appropriate questions that could come to mind. You might ask yourself, for example: "Who am I?", "Why couldn't I be different than I am now?", and "Why was I once unlike I am today?"

These are legitimate questions whose answers should be of interest to each of us. These questions are extremely relevant to the subject of this book.

The extent to which the answers are generally known is the degree to which we know each other and ourselves. Therefore it could be said, without fear of contradiction, that I have some general knowledge about you. Likewise you will know quite a bit about me, that is, once you finish reading this book.

Now let's explore each of these questions. (1) Who are you? You are the sum total of your experiences from the time of conception until the present moment. (2) Why did you come to be the way you are? You came to be the way you are because your experiences, which, conceivably similar to others, are unique. No one's total experiences are identical in every detail to those of another. (3) Why couldn't you be different than you are now? It's possible that you could be. By realizing that experiences can be both positive and negative by conscious selection of them, we can bring about changes in the way we are. (More on the selective powers of the conscious mind later). (4) Why were you not always like you are today? For the same reason that in the future you will not be exactly as you are now. We are continually undergoing changes and development from birth to death. This is of extreme significance as far as our addictions are concerned.

We came to be the way we are because of the unique hourly and daily external as well as internal influences on our growth, development, and human relations. It was actually inseparable from and interdependent upon them. We are exactly as we are because of our personal, family, work, and social relations. None of these is decisive per se but has to be considered within the overall context of development. That's why at the outset we said that we are the *sum total* of our experiences.

1. *Traditional View*

While change is universally accepted yet the traditional view differs from the modern scientific view.

The traditional outlook takes the position that change is basically evolutionary. It holds that this evolution of things, processes and phenomena does take place but things remain basically as they are. Thus they are classified, separated and placed within distinct categories. Things are either in this category or that category. Once classified into either *this* or *that*, they remain fixed within the confines of their identities and such change is independent of the change that may be taking place elsewhere.

From this view it follows that if one is addicted he is more or less filed away as an addict. He then becomes separated, classified, different. His criminal propensities stamp him as likely to inhabit jails or prisons. After all he is an addict who is outside and independent of the mainstream of society.

This type of thinking logically follows from a fixed, philosophical view that things and processes are by nature impervious to change beyond the boundaries of their identities.

For one seeking to overcome addiction it can be seen that any attempt to apply this outlook to his problem inevitably results in notions of fatalism. Why? Because if there is no change beyond the boundaries of one's identity then it logically follows that "once an addict, always an addict". It thus becomes hopeless and futile to think one can permanently defeat his addiction.

2. *Modern Scientific View*

In order to relate a realistic message to those seeking to overcome their addictions, the traditional view had to be challenged. It had to be demonstrated that the false but embedded concept was at variance with reality. It had to be shown that this is an incorrect view of exactly how universal change and development takes place.

The discoveries of America's foremost scientist, Dr. Albert Einstein demonstrated the foundations of change and how it takes place. When he advanced his atomic theory the ubiquitous nature of change was reinforced as scientific fact. He showed the atom, with its protons, electrons, and neutrons, to be in a constant state of movement; that each atom has its negative and positive forces.

If such be the case, and if atoms exist within everything throughout the universe, then it follows that nothing is without change. His discoveries further supported the theory that change can be either positive or negative according to the circumstances. This is no longer mere theory but scientific fact.

The significance of such discoveries should be readily apparent to the addict. Now he is freed from the chains of fatalism. Not only is the fact of omnipresent change reinforced but, more importantly, it can take either a positive or negative direction! It raises the appropriate question as to what can one, who is addicted, do for himself to bring about the desired change. Before we proceed to answer this question there must be an introduction to the laws that govern the manner in which this change and development is taking place before our very eyes!

The traditional view accepted part of Einstein's findings. It understood that all phenomena, things and processes are not static within their own identities. It was *outside* of these identities that the problem arose. Problems also surfaced with regard to the positive and negative change. Positively re-programming the subconscious mind, which as we will learn later, is essential to recovery from our addictions. Traditional views still cling to the incorrect notion of separating, categorizing and classifying things within *this* or *that* permanent identity. The law of interrelation virtually destroyed the separate, isolated, category theory. Scientifically it was shown that not only does everything exist in a constant and perpetual state of *becoming* but this process is not strictly within categories of identities. On the contrary it was shown that while everything is undergoing change and development, such change is inseparable from, interrelated with, and interdependent upon, the change simultaneously taking place within the surrounding phenomena and environment. Later there will be many examples of the operation of these laws in addition to the practical conclusions to be drawn from them. First, however we shall proceed to the first one.

(A). *Law of Quantity & Quality*

Basically this means that change takes place on an evolutionary basis. It is basically quantitative because movement is slow, gradual, often unnoticeable but continuous. It is qualitative also because at a definite point in time these quantitative changes give rise to something else. What's more that something else is oftentimes the opposite of what was before.

This change, unlike the evolutionary, gradual type, is revolutionary because it is sudden, abrupt and ushers in a completely new identity.

This law has tremendous significance for us and our addictions. We certainly want to change into the opposite state from what existed before; from being addicted to being non addicted. An inseparable aspect of this law is the unity of opposites. If the atom is the basic component of our bodies, nature, as well as the entire universe, then it follows that their interaction influences the course of development and the direction of change. Furthermore, it is quite understandable that these opposite forces can actually change into each other. Indeed this is what takes place. Positive replaces negative, new replaces old, etc. These opposite forces are at work within the atom as well as within all of our human experiences and are particularly important to the one seeking to overcome addiction. This first law then tells us to keep in mind that all processes and things change as a result of both their internal nature and their external influences. The internal nature is basically a contradiction. This contradiction is between what a thing is a given moment and at the same time what it is *becoming*. It is a struggle, if you will, between the old and the new. The external influences consist of the environment which, of course, includes the totality of human relationships to which one is subjected. The ability of opposites to change into each other is based on circumstances, which are usually quantitative in nature. For example, it is circumstances that can change good into bad, peace into war, love into hate, addict into non addict and so forth.

The law of quantity and quality is vital to our recovery, therefore an attempt will be made to make its operation clear by several examples.

Example 1: You desire to steam open an envelope to insert a check you forgot when paying a bill. A pot of water is drawn and placed on the kitchen stove. As the heat from the fire under it increases, a point is reached where it begins to boil and steam arises.

Here the "continuous external influence" (heat) "at a definite point in time" (boiling) gave rise to "something else" (steam) and this something else was different than "what was before". Note also that the "desire" to steam open the envelope is "consciously" deciding you want steam and "selecting" this method.

Example 2: Your friend receives a six month jail sentence for driving while intoxicated. He begins his jail sentence, therefore he is no longer free. One hundred and eighty days pass and he is released. He is now free.

In this scenario "180 days represent 'continuous external influence'" on the qualitative state of "not being free". At a definite point in time, (the last day) the existing state of not being free is changed into a "different" state of being; namely being free.

Example 3: The relationship between my wife and me is not good because I have repeatedly neglected her. I desire to improve it so I send her flowers and take her to movies regularly. The relationship becomes good.

Here, again, "repeated external influences" applied to something (bad relationship), at a definite point in time (when change is noticed) changes that something (bad relationship) into something different (good relationship). Here also the external influences were "consciously selected". This is a point of extreme importance in overcoming addictions.

There are examples throughout nature which prove this law, yet suffice it to say I trust the point is clear. In each of these examples, repetitive or "continuous external influences on something, at a definite point in time gave rise to something else". What's more the something else was different and usually "opposite" of "what was before".

It is worthy to note that in each of the examples the process could be reversed. This could be done by "consciously selecting" different "external influences". In other words by condensation, the steam could again be converted to water or if a freezer were "selected" it could be changed into ice.

In Example 2, your friend's loss of freedom could be extended beyond 180 days by the "external influences" of repeated violent behaviors.

In Example 3, I could again be the cause of my relationship deterioration by the "external influences" of repeated neglect.

We must consciously select the "external influences". This means our environment as well as our human relations. By doing so "repeatedly" and "continuously", we will inevitably be transformed from a state of addiction into happy, healthy, free people, with only addictions that are benign and harmless.

There are "internal influences" also that are germane to all change. For example, if we take an egg and place it under external conditions of incubation, those "external" conditions will at some "definite point in time" change the egg into "something else". However the something *else* can only be a chicken because of the "internal influences" or nature of the egg. Similarly, if we mix the proper ingredients of dough, place it in an oven and apply the "external" influence of heat, the mixture will, at some definite point in time, change into "something else". However this "something else" can only be bread because that's the "internal" nature of the mixture.

By the same token, in pursuing positive practices during recovery we will be able to transform "someone" suffering from addiction into "someone" free from addiction (the opposite of what was before).

This then is the lesson to be learned from embracing the correct view of how the universe actually changes and develops. Whether we realize it or not. Whether we accept it or not, this is the dynamism that is taking place before our very eyes!

To fully grasp the significance of the universal laws of change is to provide us with solid scientific direction as far as ridding ourselves of our addictions and negative habits. We are no longer strapped by unscientific notions of the status quo. The status is never quo. Things and phenomena are ceaselessly being transformed into something else, usually their opposites, on the basis of ever changing circumstances. What's good can become bad; what's new can become old; he who's honest can become dishonest; he who has an addiction can rid himself of the addiction. The controlling factor is the different circumstances or more precisely, the "conscious desire" to create different circumstances.

First, we must realize and understand that we are like the main gear in the machinery involving our addiction. It is therefore essential to shed the self centeredness that's at the core of the addicted one's personality. We must get outside ourselves by reaching out to others who have similar goals and experiences.

Second, it should be borne in mind that change is ubiquitous. It is everywhere and occurring at all times simultaneously. However, as the gears turn at different speeds, so do the various phenomena also develop and change at their own pace.

Third, never lose sight of the interrelation and interdependence of all forms of existence. In this way we distance ourselves from notions of isolation and approach our goals with humility and a sense of fellowship with those who may be struggling with their addiction.

Fourth, we should be aware and appreciative of the unique power we have that enables us to "consciously select" our thoughts and experiences. In this way we can greatly influence the course of our own development. We will thus be able to change in a positive rather than negative direction. We will be able to create circumstances that will be conducive to becoming free from addiction rather than to perpetuate our addictive lifestyle.

Fifth, by viewing things in terms of the totality of their change and development we will be approaching the problem in a scientific manner. As a result our concentration will not be on an isolated and separate aspect but will encompass the problem as a whole; that is the total circumstances. One of the most effective methods of attacking a problem is to deal with the circumstances surrounding it. This is especially productive in situations where a direct approach yields unfavorable results.

For example, the problem of addiction may be approached by abstaining cold turkey. This direct method is often unsuccessful. On the other hand changing the circumstances so as to make it temporarily impossible to obtain that on which you may be chemically dependent may be needed to sufficiently de-tox oneself. Once de-toxed, will power is restored and one can better deal with obsession that repeatedly compels one to return to the addiction. Until detoxification takes place, will power is no match for obsession.

To see things in their totality means to understand the law of interrelation which will be dealt with shortly. Two analogies will be used to demonstrate the operation of this as well as the other laws of change and development. Hopefully, as a result, the picture will be much clearer.

We begin by an impregnation of the female egg (ovum) by the male sperm. Once the sperm enters the ovum, impregnation is completed. There is then a fertilized egg which implants itself within the uterine wall. The egg consists of only one cell each with an equal number of chromosomes (24) from both father and mother (a total of 48). Within these chromosomes are genes which determine all of our future characteristics and traits. Cell division begins immediately. As the original cell splits and divides, it begins to grow. Tests at this point would prove positive. Indeed a state of pregnancy has come into existence.

Before proceeding further, let's stop at juncture and see which, if any, of the universal laws are in operation.

Certainly a state of flux exists. It is evident that there is an observable process where something has emerged (come into being) and is undergoing constant change (developing). Furthermore the change taking place is of both a quantitative and qualitative nature. It is quantitative because it is gradual and continuous. It is qualitative because new identities emerged as a result. What did these gradual, quantitative changes give rise to? What was this "something else" that was different than "what was before"? It was the emergence of specialized cells that were ultimately to be the foundation for different types of body tissue. Important also is the fact that these specialized cells came into existence as a result of the internal nature of a thing to be what it is at the moment and at the same time also be that which it is becoming. Lastly but no less significant, the changes taking place within the fertilized ovum egg are positively or negatively influenced by the existing environment within the uterus (external circumstances). This environment is interrelated with, interdependent upon and inseparable from, the physiological state of the mother.

Now let's proceed in the course of embryonic development to another stage, a higher stage, if you will.

As the specialized cells are born this new qualitative existence (identity) brings with it its own unique quantitative changes. These gradual transformations thus gave rise to something that did not exist before (tissues). The tissues become specialized to the same degree as that of the cells that gave rise to them. They are the result of the internal nature of the cells that preceded their origin. Because of this internal nature of different specialized cells to be what they are and also what they are becoming, distinct tissues and later organs come into existence. The external circumstances, including the uterine environment as well as that of the mother via the umbilical cord and placenta either positively or negatively influence this fetal development.

The internal nature of a thing is decisive only as to what it can become. In other words, specialized heart cells cannot become specialized brain cells or liver cells, nor is an incubated chicken egg capable of becoming anything other than a chicken. This is true regardless of the external (environmental) influence. External influences are significant only in the sense of changing a thing or phenomenon into what it is capable of becoming; what it *can* become. External influences can either be positive or negative. It is without question however, that external (environmental) circumstances can transform things into their opposites. A kid may be basically good but associating with bad kids can influence him to such an extent that he becomes bad. Food is good for you but repeated non-nutritional choices become bad for you. Each case is one of external circumstances.

A still higher stage in the development of the embryo is reached when organs begin to emerge. These come into existence, of course, as a result of the same type of quantitative changes that began at fertilization of the female (ovum).

Even further specialization of the cells takes place as different functions arise within each organ. The universal laws of change are operative throughout the entire process of prenatal development. The complex interrelationships during this period are evident, the interdependence upon the nervous system is observed.

Much more so than the machine with its many gears, the prenatal process contains many different tissues and organs. They are all working together. They all have their proper functions and their proper relation to the whole. Thus there is assurance that the overall process runs smoothly.

The quantitative (gradual) changes that usher in qualitative (new forms) changes are relentless. With the formation of the brain consciousness arises. Ultimately, along with positive, external, environmental circumstances the miracle of a healthy birth is celebrated.

The development begun at the time of fertilization continues within the baby beyond birth, indeed until death. The principle difference between prenatal and post natal development is the character of the external influence, the environment. Instead of external influences mainly emanating from the mother via the umbilical cord and placenta now the external influences are broadened to include those of the family. Still later they extend to other human and even animal relations.

I trust it is becoming clear as to the enormous significance the foregoing analysis holds for one seeking to overcome an addiction. If viewed in its proper perspective, then it is easy to utilize the proven method in undertaking the solution. Only then will the notions of fatalism be dispelled because things and processes will be seen in their movement, their interrelations and interdependence. This will be in opposition to the prevailing view that considers development and change to be isolated and separate from that of its surrounding circumstances. There will be no more categorizing phenomena and things as either *this* or *that* but rather will be understood that whatever exists can at the same time be changing into something else, which can be either positive or negative. This is when "conscious selection" of external influences (environment) is decisive.

(B). *Law of Contradiction*

This law is central to understanding the dynamics of change. It also contains the principles of the "unity of opposites". It is the internal content of all things, processes and phenomena. It is the key to their self movement and development. The opposites that are united in contradiction, ceaselessly struggle against each other, each striving to gain ascendancy. Positive forces are united in struggle against negative forces; conservative elements striving to maintain things as they are against forces struggling for change; the present struggling to hold on against the unyielding force of the future. The present is wedged in a vise between the past and the future. Since it is transitory and the past is history, it's the forces of the future that, despite setbacks, invariably emerges triumphant. The present must yield to the future. The old must give way to the new.

Contradictions of opposite forces are within all of our human experiences and are of particular importance to one seeking to overcome addiction. Each contradiction is between what a thing is at any given moment and what it is *becoming*. On close analysis there is most certainly to be found a positive as well as a negative aspect of whatever process is in question.

The ability of opposites within a contradiction to change into each other is based on concrete circumstances which are usually quantitative in nature. For example it is circumstances that can change good into bad, peace into war, love into hate, failure into success, happiness into unhappiness as well as addict into non addict.

(C). *Law of Interrelation*

We shall begin our first example of the law of interrelation by resorting to a somewhat mechanical analogy. From there we will proceed to one involving human relationships.

Imagine, if you will, a machine comprised of several gears of different sizes. They are all working together. They all fit into their proper grooves in order to insure that the machine runs smoothly and efficiently. They all turn at different rates of speed; the larger ones, of course, turning slower than the smaller ones. As the machine turns they each move at such speed as will enable them to fit in the respective grooves. By doing so the machine functions properly.

Now let's celebrate your birth. Your mother and father are elated over their newborn. So too are your older brothers and sisters. Days pass and your growth, change and development becomes obvious. Considering your family as the machine, you are the smallest gear that's turning and you have your own rate at which you turn. Your brothers and sisters represent gears also and they are turning at their respective rates of speed, perhaps somewhat slower than you. Finally there is your mother and father whose rate of development is probably slower than all since they represent the plateau of maturity.

All of the members "fit" into their proper "grooves" of the family machine thus insuring that it functions smoothly and efficiently. There is an interrelation and interdependence of all the members without which the family would not function smoothly and without discord.

The foregoing analogies are intended to emphasize the fact of the interrelationship and interdependence among different types of movement; also that the change constant in our lives is inseparable from, yet interrelated with and interdependent upon, that which is simultaneously taking place in our environment.

There is an important qualitative difference however, between the two analogies. While there appears to be no change within each gear in the machine (though we know there is) yet we are somewhat more aware of a change and development in our family members.

Every recovering addict has his own rate of growth, development and change. At the moment our life's paths touch we become as the gears in the machine. We fit into each other's grooves and mutually influence each other while at the same time maintaining our own individuality. Depending on the nature of the relationships that are established we are either influenced in a positive or negative manner. In the majority of cases the relationships, outside the family, are the result of our *conscious selection*. This is of extreme importance as to our relationships and to a great extent, our environment. If there is sufficiently strong desire to overcome an addiction we can consciously choose to be in the company of people who are drug free. We may even choose to engage in individual meditation. In any event, we can consciously make positive choices. The relentless change that permeates the universe and which is inherent in our being can thus assume positive direction.

We are part of the larger universe whether we admit it or try to suppress it, and the omnipresent laws operate through us just as they do throughout nature. In reality we are the highest product of nature. We are nature that thinks!

The law of interrelation further teaches us that in order to fully understand anything at any given time we must consider the circumstances and their simultaneous rate of change and development. The circumstances must, of necessity, include relations of a personal, family or social structure.

It teaches us also that change and development, far from being simple, are very complex. It includes many forms of a different nature and, like the machine gears, has many different degrees of movement.

Before proceeding with further examples and conclusions from the remaining laws, let's see what practical conclusions can be drawn from the two opposing views, namely the traditional and modern.

Thanks to the work of our country's most famous scientist, the traditional view, while still in existence, has proven to be incapable of accurately reflecting the true nature of change. We know now that not only is the universe in a constant state of flux but that this dynamism gives rise to new qualities. While matter may neither be created nor destroyed yet the forms it takes are forever changing, forever coming into existence, developing, declining and ultimately passing away, making way for new forms and infinitum.

When Einstein formulated his atomic theory, he demonstrated the constant movement within all things. The seemingly stable and motionless forms of matter (like atoms in a table for instance) are moving nonetheless. They merely give the *appearance* of being motionless and at rest. The reason is because the protons and electrons within the atoms of the table and our fingernails, for example, are moving at such a slow rate until they do not seem to be moving at all!

Certainly the conclusion to be drawn from this view differs greatly from those of the traditional outlook. There, you recall, things were viewed as fixed, categorized and separate. Under the modern view things are seen as they are, interrelated. Nothing exists in isolation but everything is interdependent upon the circumstances of its existence.

The addict therefore, is no longer considered as an anomaly, apart from the rest of society; fixed, categorized and impervious to change. It is no longer an *either-or* situation. Since things are now seen as coming into existence, growing, declining and ultimately passing away, the most important aspect of this process is not the past or even the present but *"what's becoming"*. Can it be readily seen what monumental positive applications for change exist for one suffering from addiction?

This means we no longer have to accept the notion that "once an addict, always an addict". Since a thing can now be both itself and at the same time "what it's becoming", it is possible for an addict to actually be a *recovering* addict *simultaneously*! In other words it is no longer an either-or situation. Furthermore, as pointed out earlier that things tend to change into their opposites, it can be seen that the addict can actually *become* the non-addict. This is precisely what takes place in recovery!

I trust the importance of understanding the different viewpoints and their practical application to those seeking to overcome their addictions has become clear.

The past is important for the lessons that can be learned. The present, of course is very important. However neither is as important as "what's becoming"! It is said that the mark of maturity is the ability to "sacrifice the immediate for the long range".

No longer is one who seeks to overcome addiction bound by the fatalistic approach of hopelessness from the discredited "fixed" view of things.

Now there is hope. There is a new found path out of the quagmire of addiction. By knowledge and application of the modern scientific view of change and development we can become truly free!

Using the Weapon

The purpose of the foregoing explanation was to demonstrate the operation of the universal laws of change and development that permeate all things and processes throughout the universe.

The main highlight in this exposition was to show that the most unstable factor in the equation of change is the quantitative, gradual and often imperceptive environmental influences. Sometimes they are personal, oftentimes they include the family and social relations.

It is extremely important and significant for one seeking to overcome an addiction to understand that these decisive environmental experiences are largely under his conscious control. This enables one to choose those experiences and relations that would further his goal of changing himself from an existence of addiction to a state of recovery.

Perhaps it may appear that, from time to time, I may seem to wax overly philosophical. This is understandable. Not only that but it is essential. It is essential because of the practical implications implicit in the word "philosophy".

Webster says philosophy is "the study of the fundamental truths of life and the universe". This is what we're dealing with in this book.

Furthermore it can be seen that having an effective philosophy means having one that accurately reflects reality. It must reflect reality not as we perceive it to be but as it actually is. It must be independent of our perceptions to the extent that our perceptions are incorrect. If on the other hand they are correct, that is an entirely different matter. In this case our perceptions merge with objective reality and thus we have truth.

Never before has such a weapon, so effective, been available to the addict to use in his struggle to overcome addiction. Never before has he been free to discount with confidence the false notion that "once an addict, always an addict". Such an erroneous notion was based on the outdated and discredited philosophy that held "all things and processes had identified entities and whatever change took place was bound by the limits of those entities".

Armed with a correct philosophical understanding of exactly how change and development proceed, we should seek to cultivate positive thoughts as well as positive experiences on an hourly and daily basis. By doing so we know that these gradual, hardly noticeable actions will at some point bring about a very noticeable and (qualitative) change in our attitudes and behavior. It will be different than before. The changes, if positive, will ultimately transform our attitudes, habits and behavior into the opposite of what they were before.

If on the other hand our thoughts and experiences are of a negative nature, change will nonetheless take place. The difference is that it will be a change in the level or degree of our addiction. Instead of positive attitudes, which flow from positive thoughts and experiences, we will have decidedly deeper negative attitudes and behavior.

If a state of negativity already exists additional negative input will nonetheless change it but the change, inasmuch as it already is of a negative nature, will have the effect of further deepening or exacerbating the situation.

For example we know that one suffering from a harmful addiction is lacking in the basic spiritual qualities of selfishness, humility, acceptance, honesty and love among others.

If we entertain positive thoughts and cultivate positive relationships the spiritual qualities will again surface. We will become unselfish, humble, honest and loving and less resentful.

If we entertain negative thoughts and pursue negative relationships the spiritual qualities that we lack will not remain the same nor will they disappear. They will assume a different form. They will deepen. We will become more selfish, more dishonest, and more resentful.

The point here is that the universal law of change is in effect in both cases. Remember that the status is never "quo". Things are always in contradiction with themselves. They are once *themselves* but also that which they are *becoming*.

Whether we, as addicts, become more deeply addicted because of negative thoughts and experiences or whether we begin to recover from our addiction because of positive drug free thoughts and relationships, depends in the final analysis, upon ourselves. It depends upon our *conscious selection* and the emotions that accompany this conscious selection.

Now that the universal laws of change and development have been explained, it remains to be seen just how they work to actually bring about the desired change in our lives.

We must assume the important decision has been made to overcome our addiction. What practical steps then must be taken to attain our goal?

First we must keep in mind that the subconscious is the seat of our habits, remember that it must be reprogrammed.

Remember also that all successful treatment programs and treatment centers fashion their programs toward this end.

To understand how the subconscious is reprogrammed by all successful treatment programs, your attention is directed to the "garden analogy" in the next chapter. Hopefully then it will be much clearer.

The fact that a decision has been made to recover from our addictions means that we will "consciously select" thoughts and experiences that will be positive and not drug oriented. These, hopefully, will consist of daily meditation and regular group meetings. Along with this new behavior will come new relationships and new interests.

We will see how the "conscious selection" of the positive practices is like seeds that are planted in a regular garden. The difference being, namely, that with respect to our subconscious mind, the process is a continuous and ongoing one.

As they take root the inexorable law of quantitative and qualitative development governs their process of growth. The regular and continuous positive experiences result in the emergence of drug free attitudes, they are different and the exact opposite of those that existed before treatment began.

Attitudes of sharing replace selfishness; honesty replaces dishonesty; humility replaces arrogance; anger and resentment give way to love and acceptance.

Since these new thoughts and experiences are emotionally charged with a faithful commitment, they readily take root in the "garden" of our subconscious. The result of these positive practices is new behavior patterns. To be emotionally charged means they must be accompanied with strong feelings of belief.

These patterns, born from our subconscious reprogramming, have a dynamic of their own. They are cultivated from our subconscious garden. Once grown, they reinforce the positive practices from which they came. Further growth is manifested in cementing new relationships and new interests which are *outside* the group fellowship.

Thus they become the basis for an entirely different way of life for us. It is a new life, one that replaces the old. It is the exact opposite of our life of addiction, it's a life of true happiness.

We then become, to paraphrase some important words; "Free at last! Free at last! We're grateful to our higher power, we're free at last!"

The Subconscious & Spirituality

An introduction to the subconscious mind is perhaps the single most important issue with regard to overcoming addictions. This is so because it is without a doubt the seat of all of our habits and addictions.

Spirituality is an integral part of the process because it is virtually impossible to defeat addictions without a re-awakening of certain spiritual principles.

What are these principles? They are, above all, honesty, love, unselfishness, gratitude, forgiveness, patience, tolerance, and humility among others.

The subconscious must be reprogrammed with spiritual principles and attitudes for those who are addicted to recover. Since this is so we shall begin by understanding the conscious and subconscious mind, the different functions of each and their interaction.

The famous Schick program was in the forefront of the recognition that the subconscious is the seat of our habits and addictions. All programs however, are designed to reach and influence it. Even the most effective ones do not, in my opinion, put sufficient emphasis on the importance of reprogramming the subconscious. There is nothing more important to one in recovery than a full and complete understanding of the function of the subconscious.

In my first book *"Crack, You and Your Love Ones"*, I pointed out that few people truly understand the function of the subconscious in our daily lives. Indeed I, for quite some time, did not appreciate the fact that for practical purposes we actually have not one but *two* minds! This may sound far fetched but further explanation will make the point clear.

For functional purposes there are really two minds existing within each individual. One is the conscious and the other is the subconscious. One is the tip of the iceberg, so to speak, and the other is its base. The subconscious is by far the dominant of the two as far as our behavior is concerned. As will be explained later in detail, the subconscious appears to have its physiological origin in the autonomic nervous system whereas the conscious mind emanates from the activity of the brain, each has separate functions but both are inseparable. In the interest of clarity allow me to make an analogy.

Imagine, if you will, a gardener as he goes about the business of tending his garden. During the planting time he obtains the specific types of seeds he wants and plants them. Let's say he wants to cultivate okra, beets and cabbage. He purchases okra and beet seeds but mistakenly plants broccoli instead of the cabbage seeds. When they begin to grow he realizes he doesn't have what he intended. Regardless of how strong his desire for cabbage or how efficient his gardening skills may be he, nevertheless, will only be able to get okra, beet and broccoli crop. The answer is obvious. "We reap what we sow".

In this analogy the gardener is the conscious mind. The subconscious mind is the garden. The conscious mind, like the gardener, has the power of "selection". It can select the thoughts and experiences it "wants" to plant in the subconscious garden. Once planted they are nurtured, cultivated and ultimately realized in our attitudes and behavior. This is so because the conscious and subconscious have separate and distinct functions. What are they?

The conscious mind has the duty to reason, plan, judge and analyze. It also has the unique power of being able to "choose" what is received by the subconscious. Therefore it can be said that it is in the driver's seat as far as what thoughts and experiences (seeds) are introduced into the garden. This unique power of the conscious mind is the most *decisive* factor in overcoming the disease of addiction.

The subconscious mind has an entirely different function. It regulates our heart rate; body temperature, digestion, blood pressure, dreams, attitudes, reactions, habits and ultimately our behavior.

Whereas the conscious mind is active only during our waking hours, the subconscious is working twenty four hours a day from the day we are born to the day we die. In order to control our dreams it would, of necessity, have to operate during sleep. Further in order to regulate behavior it would, of necessity, have to be the seat of our habits and addictions because they are merely behavior patterns.

Also if through our conscious mind we are about to "select" our thoughts and if the subconscious will ultimately act them out then it follows that we are not only capable of ridding ourselves of our addiction but, more importantly, we are capable of determining our own destiny!

Now that we have discussed the relation between conscious and the subconscious as regards our addictions, it remains for us to see and appreciate the definite link between the subconscious and spirituality.

From the immemorial, regardless of one's religious beliefs, it has been generally recognized by man that there is some "force" governing the universe; regulating the seasons, etc. Man and all forms of organic as well as inorganic matter is an integral part of this "force".

Spirituality is defined as "life giving force" and things of "a sacred matter". I might add that what is spiritual somehow has the connotation of being "mysterious", "noble" and often "unexplainable".

According to one viewpoint the space between thought of the brain and the chemical produced by it is the "spirit", the "you", if you will. The unique "force" that initiates the thought. The subconscious mind, this "you" or "force" is existing within each of us and is our spiritual connection with the universal "force" governing the universe. It is definitely "mysterious", "unexplainable" and "divine" in its nature. It's not only involved in our behavior but it influences our station in life; whether we succeed or fail; whether we are productive or non-productive.

I'm convinced that there is a non-biblical secular message to the phrase, "Seek ye the kingdom of God" and the "Kingdom of God is within you". In my opinion this is definitely alerting us to the powerful spiritual force within each of us called the subconscious. When properly understood and positively programmed by the "selective" power of our conscious mind there are limitless horizons we can conquer!

The point is to educate people in general and those suffering from the disease of addiction in particular, to the powerful and decisive role of the subconscious in ridding ourselves of our unwanted habits. This is the single most important element lacking in the treatment programs of today. Even the most successful ones should openly emphasize to their patients that the main purpose is to reprogram the subconscious mind. Once this is understood, the person can assist the practitioner in whatever program he may be involved in by helping himself. It would make it easier for both and greatly increase the rate of successful rehabilitation.

An entire book could be written on the subconscious mind and behavior; no doubt many have. For some reason very few people struggling with addictions are aware of this important connection. With the rise in the level of drug use throughout the nation it is imperative that there also be a rise in the level of understanding of this connection.

The key to solving the drug crisis in our country lies in reducing the demand and not supply. Once the demand for illegal drugs is gone so will go the drug dealers. It is my firm belief that a thorough understanding of the role of the subconscious with respect to addiction would dramatically reduce the amount of addicts.

Since at least eighty percent of the inmates in our prisons are there for drug related crimes, the first noticeable impact would be the immediate availability of jail space. The need for additional jails would not be nearly as acute. The money saved could be used to expand treatment centers and rehabilitation programs.

Speaking of books written on the application of the subconscious as it relates to behavior, none I've read is better than "The Power of Positive Thinking", by Norman Vincent Peale. This famous best seller was certainly in the forefront of those I read on the subject. I'm sure there are others, but this one in particular looms large in my mind.

However, regardless of the previous works and the number of them there is a need now more then ever to be informed as to the role of the subconscious in solving the problem of addiction. In other words information should be available to all as to how the subconscious works and its role in our attitudes, addictions, and behavior. There is a definite void in the area that is crying out to be filled as our nation struggles for solutions to the drug epidemic from which, it seems, we are unable to extricate ourselves. A powerful weapon in this struggle has been overlooked by our failure to make the general public aware of this vital connection.

It would be interesting and, I believe, very surprising to know, through a national poll, just how many people know how the subconscious is the ultimate regulator of our habits and behavior. In particular it would be revealing to know how many suffering from addiction are aware that it is *impossible* to overcome it without reprogramming the subconscious. Making this knowledge generally known would produce positive results of mammoth proportions as far as controlling and reducing the demand for illegal drugs in our country.

This connection is a picture that should constantly be kept in mind. By doing so the addicted person is standing at the door of recovery. He needs only to open it and enter.

What is this picture? I shall attempt to paint it by showing the relationships between humanity and the universe.

Even modern psychology recognizes the existence of some kind of "force" that regulates the universe and of which man is, of course, an integral part.

Some religions personify this force by calling it "God". Some Eastern philosophers do not personify it and instead refer to it as the "Mystic Law".

In the scientific community it is often referred to as "nature" with its laws of "cause and effect". Whatever we call it the result is the same. The main common denominator of all is the acceptance of a force more powerful and more influential than any human being. By whatever name, one thing we know, it governs the entire universe and all within it. We see the evidence daily as night follows day and the seasons come and go with unerring certainty. One might say the actions of this "force" triggers a reaction on the part of the universe to it. One being the "cause" and the other the "effect".

In painting the picture of this relation between this "force" and our "subconscious minds", I shall use the analogies consisting of two basic substances; air and water.

The universal nature of this "force" could certainly be reflected in the air. The infinite atoms that pervade the atmosphere are truly omnipresent. They are everywhere. Every form of existence in both the plant and animal kingdoms draw upon air in order to sustain life. Every time we breathe we demonstrate this inseparable connection. There exists an interdependence without which human life would be impossible. During our waking hours we are keenly conscious of this interdependence. Our conscious mind tells us that the connection is undeniable.

Bear in mind here that we are talking about the "tip" of the "iceberg". The tip represents the conscious mind whose function it is to reason, judge, plan, analyze and make judgments.

Though we're aware of this connection between the "universal force" and our "conscious mind" during our waking hours, what about when we are not aware of it? What about when we are asleep? Does the connection exist? Is it different? If so, in what way?

These questions go to the heart of the matter as far as addiction is concerned and I shall attempt to answer them.

Of course the connection still exists when we are asleep. This is so simply because we have to breathe during sleep as well as when we are awake. However it does not exist in the same form as before. Now the relationship is with that non-waking part of our mind, the "base of the iceberg", which is our subconscious. As previously mentioned, it has an entirely different function than that of our conscious mind. Recall, if you will, that it is incapable of thinking, analyzing, planning and making judgments. Instead it regulates our body functions including digestion and heartbeat, and finds expression in our dreams. The connection between the universal force and the subconscious are "mystical" in nature. They are most powerful in their effect on our lives yet we, for the most part, are entirely unaware of the operation in spite of the fact that it is continuously working twenty four hours a day. It is because of our unawareness of this powerful "force" in our lives that the subconscious assumes a "divine", "mystical" and "spiritual" character. It essentially operates in silence just as the seeds grow silently in the garden! By means of it we can identify with the omnipotence of the universal "force" and draw upon its power. If the subconscious draws its power from this source then it is understandable for such to be beyond the ordinary power of the conscious mind.

The most important aspect of the conscious mind, you will recall, is its power of "selection". It will be dealt with further because of its relation to the subconscious in successfully overcoming our undesirable addictions. In our garden analogy the conscious mind with its selective power is tantamount to "keeper of the garden gate". Nothing reaches the subconscious except through it.

Hopefully by means of our "air" analogy the picture of the connection between the universal "force" and the conscious and subconscious has become somewhat clearer; however for the sake of an even better picture our next analogy will involve an equally basic substance namely "water".

The universal "force" can be likened to a river. We know that by constructing dams electric power can be created. A river can and often does serve to irrigate land by means of tributaries that branch off as it flows along its path. Tributary or branch is a connecting link between the river and the land to be irrigated. Consider, if you will the river to be the universal "force" and each tributary a connecting link to a subconscious garden to be irrigated.

If we recall the analogy where the seeds of thought and experiences are planted in the subconscious garden the picture should become clearer. Also we can appreciate the role of the conscious mind as the "keeper of the garden gate". The "keeper" selects the seeds of thought to be planted in the garden; however once they are planted the tributaries from the universal "force" (river) water them. The most important point to keep in mind is just like real seeds, these thoughts and experiences will come forth in silence from the subconscious and flourish exactly as would real seeds. Furthermore if they are positive thoughts of success we will be successful; if they are negative thoughts and attitudes, inevitably we will fail; if they are thoughts and experiences that are drug oriented we will become thoroughly addicted; and if they are drug free and non addictive thoughts and experiences, we will be successful in our recovery.

Our subconscious has no power of selection. It only *acts* on what it receives. This power of selection is the exclusive function of the conscious mind. By means of it the subconscious is programmed. The conscious mind then is the "great programmer", a point we should never lose sight of as far as addiction is concerned. The only way to assure continued successful recovery is to have an ongoing positive plan of programming the subconscious because it is virtually impossible to reason away a habit. It is also highly improbable to "will" away a habit. This is so because, in addiction, the element of "obsession" is dominant over "will power". It is obsession that repeatedly returns us to our drug of choice. Once we return then "compulsion" drives us to indulge in excess. This is especially true of an addict or one with an addictive personality. Once started he is unable to stop. This is why it is said in the literature of narcotics anonymous that "one is too many and a thousand are not enough".

All successful treatment programs, without exception, have a practical plan of reprogramming the subconscious. If this were not the case they would not be successful. The subconscious *must* be reprogrammed with positive anti-addictive thoughts simply because it is the seat of our habits.

I feel strongly that if those being treated were made aware of the role of the subconscious and understood the relation between it and their conscious mind, they could greatly facilitate their own recovery. Although such programs as Alcoholics Anonymous and Narcotics Anonymous are tested and proven there are practical steps one can take as an individual to combat the process of addiction. In fact it is entirely possible for one, armed with knowledge of how the subconscious can be influenced by the conscious mind, to overcome his addiction without entering a treatment program. While this is possible, it is highly improbable and some sort of treatment program is recommended, especially after the beginning stage of recovery.

How can one overcome his addiction without entering a treatment program? More precisely, what practical steps could be taken by the individual to reprogram his subconscious mind?

It is done mainly by means of verbal affirmations. To "affirm", Webster says, is to "state emphatically". In other words when we emphasize and stress that which we say, then we "affirm". So when we speak to ourselves with "feeling" and "emphasis" we are engaging in verbal affirmations. Such is the case when we repeat aloud the Lord's Prayer or any other thoughts with feeling and faith.

Now let's see how this applies to the above question "What steps could be taken to reprogram the subconscious by the individual?"

We already know that through our conscious mind we can select our thoughts. In order to do this we merely need to concentrate on that which we want to think about. The ideal way to do this is by meditation; by retreating to a quiet place where in our solitude, we are free from unwanted distractions.

The conscious mind (garden) then selects the thoughts (seeds) to be planted in the subconscious (garden). Remember that thoughts which eventually take root in the subconscious are those accompanied with *feeling, faith* and *emphasis*. The gardener with the green thumb is the one who *believes* in himself.

A practical application could go something like this: "I firmly feel that I'm about to turn my life around. Nothing but jails, institutions, and death are ahead for me by continuing to use drugs. I truly see a better life and I deserve a better life. I'm tired of being dishonest with myself and I see myself changing into my opposite. I know I can once again take control of my life. I have a strong feeling that it is again becoming organized. Dope is for dopes and when you use you lose. I'm a winner. I've always been a winner. Just got off the track and that's life. The important thing is that I am now getting back on track. I am not concerned about the past because that has come and gone. The experience of using, although detrimental as it was, has made me place a high value on being clean. Therefore I do not regret it because I was not responsible for being addicted. I'm becoming clean but I'm also becoming serene.

I'll not dwell on what happened before because that is no more. I am in the process now of preparing myself for the future because after all that is really what's important. It is even more important than the present since each tick of the clock leaves the present behind and brings forth the future. I know that this is the key to shedding those destructive attitudes and habits that were once a part of me. I'm leaving them behind. I'm discarding them because, through my power of meditation and thought selection, I am planting the seeds of positive thought in my subconscious mind. I have faith in the power of my subconscious to accept these seeds and bring them to bloom and fruition. I know that it is true that we reap what we sow in life. I know without a doubt that the positive thoughts given to my subconscious mind will be received and acted upon in the form of drug free behavior, thus I am reshaping my destiny"!

This is an example of verbal affirmation. There can be as many variations as there are individuals who practice them. As long as they are with feeling and conviction they will be received and acted on by the subconscious.

The main prerequisite to embarking upon a program of recovery is the desire to do so. After that comes conscious "selection". Thousands throughout the country (maybe millions) need to rid themselves of their addictions. No amount of preaching as to the dangers of their habits will do any good. The path to a new and rewarding life is now, more than ever, open to them. However the key is that they must have to "will".

As you speak during meditation you must literally "see" yourself becoming the person you want to be. However, you shouldn't say "I *want* to become drug free" but rather "I *am* becoming drug free".

These affirmations should be made on a daily basis, preferably in the quiet retreat of solitude. Thus in this way we establish contact with our subconscious mind and are able to furnish it with the seeds of thought it needs to eventually usher forth a change in our behavior.

An extension of this method is also employed in treatment programs. When there are reading sessions from the big book of "A.A." and when the benefits of being clean are shared by members of Narcotics Anonymous at their discussion meetings, they are in effect reprogramming the subconscious by means of verbal affirmations. The fact that they don't stress this to their members does not make it any less true that this is what exactly happens. In all fairness to these programs I must admit that they do refer to the subconscious mind from time to time. It would be glaringly contradictory if they did not.

To truly appreciate the role our subconscious plays in determining our actions one needs only to observe another sleeping. Of course this should be done over a relative extended period of time, say thirty minutes or more. The activity of the subconscious will cause the person to change positions from time to time. However, regardless of how active or inactive a person may be physically during sleep, he or she invariably finds a certain position that appears most comfortable to them. This is the position that the subconscious has been programmed over time to accept as conducive to restful sleep for that particular person. This is always the position that each individual will spend the most time in during sleep. Some are more restful on their side, others seem to prefer sleeping on their stomachs, while still others find more comfort sleeping on their backs. In any event whatever position they are in it is the one that the subconscious has been programmed to act out. It is their particular habit of sleeping.

The Environment

Environmental (external, repetitive, continuous, quantitative) practices and attitudes are the most decisive factors influencing the direction (positive or negative) of change and development.

Therefore this must be our area of emphasis and since there are many, we will undertake to become aware of them.

First of all, speaking of environment in general, it could be said that while our environment certainly influences us the fact is we can, to a limited extent, also influence our environment. However, there is a definite difference in the degree of influence. Miscalculation of this degree of difference certainly strongly contributed to my relapse. Being clean, I thought I would be able to persuade those still using to abstain by my example. I failed to realize that the influence of the environment upon me was much stronger, in the long run, than my influence to bring about changes in it.

At a group session I attended the speaker gave the following example which somewhat diminished my cockiness and cause me to place the two influences (environmental and individual) in proper perspective.

I was at a group meeting and mentioned to them that I often visited places and people who were still using and even while they were using there was no desire whatsoever in *me* to use. I told them that I was firmly convinced, in my own mind, that under no circumstances, would I ever use again.

The speaker told me that I was on the wrong path and while I was currently resisting the urge to use, still it was only a matter of time before I did, this is the scenario he gave:

He said, "You enter a room filled with people. The room temperature is very high. At best their clothing consists of short sleeves and other lightweight types. You have on an overcoat since it was cold outside. When asked to remove it you decline to do so yet you remain in the room for quite awhile. You leave and return to the same room on several occasions. Eventually the heat in the room will take its toll and you'll find yourself (subconsciously) removing your coat. You'll do so without ever being aware of so!"

The environment can subject us to temptations that we feel we can effectively resist. We certainly can resist for a period of time because we consciously *intend* to do so. However that is not the issue. What is the key issue? Yes, you're right; the subconscious mind is the key here because it is the controlling factor which determines our reactions, attitudes, behavior and habits.

How many times have you heard a story similar to this? "I made up my mind that I was going to stop smoking. For six months I went about my life without a cigarette; then one day I had just finished a good meal. I walked into the bedroom and there was a cigarette my wife left burning in the ashtray. Before I knew it I picked it up and took a drag from it. I don't know for the life of me *why* I did it but I do know that ever since then I've been smoking again.

This is a typical example of how the subconscious directs our actions and reactions oftentimes against our conscious will.

Environmental influences can sometimes be extreme even tragic, such was the situation related to me by a very nice mild mannered man about to begin serving a fifty year sentence for murder.

It involved crack cocaine, but he never used, sold it or better yet, didn't even know what it looked like! How, you might ask, could he receive such a sentence based on crack cocaine and wouldn't even recognize it if he saw it? Here's the story: *A* is a single middle aged man. He has a good job, his own home, a car and is living moderately well. He meets *B*, a young woman to whom he is drawn with much feeling and affection. Unaware to *A*, *B* is addicted to smoking crack and conceals that from *A*. Repeatedly *A* experiences burglaries at his home while at work; at first he has no reason to suspect *B* and the break-ins continue over an extended period of time. *B* tells *A* she's leaving town for a couple of days to visit her mother. The next day *A* goes to the neighborhood bar and is having a beer when he looks ahead in the mirror and sees B about to enter behind him. She sees him but doesn't realize he sees her. Quickly she retreats and disappears.

When *A* returns home it has been burglarized again. When he sees her the next day and asks her about it she claims she just got back in town. When he says he saw her the day before while at the bar she becomes arrogant. She admits she broke in because she's addicted to crack and needed money. In fact, she becomes unusually aggressive and demands more money. When he tells her the only money he has is for the house payment, she becomes violent and literally thrusts her hand into his pocket. A struggle ensues. A pistol is within reach on top of the chest of drawers. Subconsciously, without thinking he grabs it and fires all six bullets into her body!

A had no criminal record and doesn't even remember reaching for the pistol nor shooting her! He received a fifty year aggravated sentence. At the time he was 55 years old.

A tragic but true account of the combined power of environmental influence and the subconscious mind!

I am often amused when people tell me what their reactions would be under circumstances of crisis or extreme stress. The truth is they really don't know what they would do. At best they *think* they know. It is not our conscious mind but our subconscious mind that determines what our reaction will be.

Earlier it was pointed out that the subconscious and conscious minds have entirely different functions. The main one of the conscious mind, we recall, was that of selection. By this process it influences and determines what ultimately reaches our subconscious.

In a much broader sense the environment also supplies fertile seeds; experiences that find their way into our subconscious. Any treatment program essentially creates an environment of many positive experiences. These include new people, interests and activities as well as attitudes. This is why they are so successful in their recovery rate. Through their programs they are in essence, reprogramming the subconscious minds of those who enter their programs. Were it otherwise they would not be successful. They would not be successful because its established and verified that it's impossible to shed an addiction without going to the seat of the problem.

Important to note is that environmental influences can be either positive or negative. The subconscious can not discriminate on this basis. It can only discriminate on the basis of those thoughts and experiences accompanied by feelings of faith, belief and confidence. These are the ones that take root and are acted upon.

Strong feelings of loneliness, anger, selfishness and arrogance are to be avoided as much as possible because while they are strong emotions and therefore likely to be acted upon by the subconscious yet they are negative.

Our environment played a key role in the origin of our addiction. The first thing that should be clear is that its origin was not sudden but rather a gradual process. Whereas we might think our addiction comes to us all at once yet we would have to admit that various external circumstances led to its birth. Furthermore these external (environmental) circumstances were of a repetitive, continuous, quantitative nature since they occurred over a period of time. Thus the universal law of quantitative and qualitative change was in operation. In other words a series of continuous experiences of a negative nature entered the subconscious and at a definite point in time changed its nature from a non addictive to an addictive state.

They consisted of new relationships, new interests, and new places. We began to do different things.

Like the external heat applied to the egg in the incubator the continuous influences began to transform the essential nature of our being. What's more it began to transform it into its opposite.

Furthermore, if the origin of our disease can be determined then it stands to reason that we should be able to follow its course of development. We know everything or process that comes into being, by necessity, undergoes a period of growth and development. Addictions are no exception to this universal law.

How then does the development of our addiction proceed once it comes into existence? Its growth and development are governed by the same law that gave rise to its birth. It is subjected to both external and internal factors.

The external factor, of course, is the surrounding circumstances which are basically environmental. This influence can be likened to the heat applied to the incubator or the oven. However just as in the case of the egg and the dough, there is an internal factor of development. This internal factor is decisive as to what it is *capable* of changing into. No amount of external influence can transform anything into something of which it is *incapable*. Heat applied to dough results only in bread. The internal factor of our environment can only change us from one to the other. If we expose ourselves to negative, drug oriented experiences we will be influenced by them and our development will proceed as that of addiction.

On the other hand if we enter a treatment program, develop new interests and relationships of a non drug oriented character, then we will become free and not addicted.

What's important is that the process is in a constant state of flux. It is in an ongoing state of continued motion. At all times the process is subject to positive and negative influences. These influences, as previously noted, are often under the direct control of the individual conscious mind through its unique "power of selection." Through faith in our higher power and ourselves we can effectively determine or change the course of our development wherever there is a strong commitment to do so.

The outmoded *either-or* concept that categorizes phenomena and things as *this* or *that* falls into disrepute. No longer do we have to accept the fatalistic view that our station in life is predetermined and unchanging. We now know, thanks to modern scientific discoveries, that we have the capability, through the awesome power of our subconscious mind, to determine not only our reactions, habits, attitudes and behavior, but more importantly, we find ourselves in the comforting position to be able to truly fashion our destiny.

Relapse

The same universal laws pervade the process of relapse that exists during the recovery period. Also like recovery, relapse has its different stages. There is partial relapse and total relapse. Neither represents absolute failure on the part of the addict to overcome the addiction. Partial relapse can actually be classified as a "slip." It exists when one partially relapses yet he or she continues the pattern of the recovery program. It is merely an interruption or temporary setback. There is a feeling of despair and lowered self esteem, but it is rapidly recognized that salvation lies in immediately returning to the program of recovery initially undertaken. Total relapse, on the other hand, is when the person completely discontinues every part of the recovery program that was originally begun. In neither case, partial or total, should the individual give up and be resigned to the notion that all is lost and that he is hopelessly addicted for life. Partial or total, relapse can at best be only temporary setbacks if a firm determination exists to rid oneself of addiction.

There are three reasons that come to mind as why one in recovery would fall victim to a relapse. (1) Lack of sustained firm determination, (2) an improper method, and (3) faulty judgment.

No amount of treatment will produce ongoing positive results if the determination to overcome addiction is diminished or weakened. During recovery the subconscious is continually receiving positive thoughts and experiences. The universal law of quantitative and qualitative change operates to maintain the recovery process. Without a sustained determination non-spiritual feelings and attitudes can creep back into our consciousness and derail our recovery. What are these feelings and attitudes? Arrogance, resentment, cockiness, despair and loneliness among others.

If sufficient desire exists these feelings and attitudes will not disrupt our program. Instead there will be the spiritual principles of humility, acceptance, hope and sharing.

To truly "want" to fashion a new life and shed our addictions is the indispensable key to success. It is far from easy to effectively reprogram our subconscious in a positive manner but it is a virtual impossibility to do so without an unswerving commitment.

The second reason we may fall victim to a relapse is that an ineffective method may be used. Any ineffective and improper method is one that violates the universal laws of change and development. In particular I'm referring to the law of quantitative change. Being the one governing the process of all development, it is the one that must be addressed when intended goals are not met or setbacks occur.

If something goes wrong during our process of recovery it's a veritable certainty to involve the repetitive, continuous and gradual quantitative experiences and thoughts used to reprogram our subconscious. In our recovery these experiences are, by necessity, positive. However the fact that a relapse has occurred is proof, per se, that negatives have entered the picture. What's more these negatives have their origin in our environment. Therefore we will know almost immediately what the problem is and also what steps to take to solve it, that is unless we suffer from faulty judgment.

Let's take an example. I had begun attending narcotics anonymous (N/A) meetings and had incorporated the first, second and third steps in my recovery program.

I was a serene, rejuvenated and very happy person. However I relapsed into that lazy leisure of lethargy and thought all was well. I had triumphed over my addiction! Never would I use again! I saw no need for a fourth step. After all hadn't I admitted to being powerless over my addiction? Hadn't I admitted that my life had become unmanageable? And that there was a power greater than I to whom I was willing to turn over my life? I was happy in the midst of my new found fellowship of N.A. I know I suffered from an incurable disease which was powerful, patient and progressive and fatal. Theoretically I accepted this but as a practical matter I went about my life as if my problem were completely solved. The notion didn't come to me that it was merely arrested. Instead of steadfastly manifesting my powerlessness I became all powerful (in my mind). I began to become irregular in attending the meetings. In my flawed judgment there was no further need for me to attend them.

What was needed, I thought, was to persuade the many people I knew to make a commitment and enter some kind of treatment program, especially N.A.

I wanted them to experience the transformation that had changed me into my opposite; from a spiritually drained individual into a drug free and serene human being.

Instead of going to meetings I began frequenting my former drug using associates. They were amazed and ashamed to see me come around often and tell them they could be like me; that they didn't have to use. I constantly reminded them that there was a proven way out. After all wasn't I a living witness?

Little did I realize that because of those repeated trips to my old environment and former "friends", I was violating one of the most fundamental laws of governing the universe. The consequences would be unwelcome to say the least.

The universal law operates with mathematical certainty in a negative sense as it does in a positive way.

The positive quantitative changes brought about by regularly attending N.A. meetings were totally environmental and included the new relationships and interests of the fellowship. I was happy and serene in my recovery because the positive environment experiences were entering my subconscious mind and reprogramming it. They were really received by my subconscious because, since I had faith in the program, they were charged with emotion.

However, by discontinuing the meetings and returning to try and persuade my old friends to enter a program, I subjected my subconscious to different environmental influences which were negative and drug oriented. Since these too, were emotionally charged (I believed and had faith I could succeed) they were also readily received by my subconscious. Instead of changing the "people", "places" and "things", I repeatedly visited, I was changed myself because ultimately I began to use again. I lost sight of the fact that my addiction is a disease that is not only powerful but patient. I learned the hard way that anyone who fails to control his environment (if addicted) will, in turn, most certainly be controlled by it.

The control of one's environment is essential to staying clean. This is perhaps the greatest challenge of all. This is mainly because of the powerful influence of a factor called "environmental cue-ins." The most obvious ones to which I subjected myself were old friends, old places and old things. When I revisited them and attempted to rescue them from their plight I was "cued-in" to my previous drug environment.

The effect of environmental cue-ins has been demonstrated by a San Francisco clinic well in the forefront of crack addiction treatment. Their experiments consisted of monitoring the blood pressure and heart rate of recovering addicts. In one case the subject would be shown different scenes flashing across a movie screen. There would be a scene of a picnic, perhaps children playing and maybe people fishing. Then suddenly a scene containing drugs and drug paraphernalia would appear and the subjects' blood pressure, breathing, and heart rate would rise sharply.

In another situation the subject would be taken on a ride to the neighborhood where he once purchased crack. Even before reaching the area (in fact as it was approached) his pulse, breathing and heart rate quickened!

This involved people who had been in treatment and with clean time as long as a year. The conclusions arrived at was that environmental cue-ins are the single strongest barrier to overcome in order for one to sustain continued success in recovery.

My personal experiences prove to me that such a conclusion is entirely correct. While there are many factors that enter into developing a relapse none is more worthy of concern than the environmental "cue-ins." This is because they are the last barrier to overcome to truly cement our ongoing successful recovery. One falsely believes all is well and that he is on a regular path of rehabilitation only to find himself in an environment partaking of a drug oftentimes before he's even consciously aware of it.

The third reason usually involved in relapse has to be faulty judgment. This was experienced by me following my first successful effort at re-programming my subconscious through meditation.

At the time I was living in the upper middle class area of Baldwin Hills in Los Angeles. Four of us, including my wife, shared a four bedroom house. We were not merely users, but addicts. There is a distinction between one who merely uses and one suffering from an addiction. It's a distinction that's very important in terms of its consequences. It will be recalled that "obsession" was the mental magnet that from time to time drew one back to his drug of choice. Also it was mentioned that once we succumbed to that first fix, "compulsion" would set in. This "compulsion", in one addicted, triggers an allergic physical response which renders us powerless to stop. On the other hand if one is merely a user and not addicted there is the will power to stop after that first hit. In the addict will power is no match for obsession and compulsion.

We were all addicted and used almost all day every day. I had recently been introduced to Buddhism by my son and daughter. They told me if I chanted daily with faith and sincerity to the Gohonzon (God of my understanding) for 90 days, that which I desired would come to pass.

I had received my Gohonzon at a meeting and had it enshrined in my newly purchased "boutsadon" and mounted on the east wall complete with candles, incense, water and fruit.

My belief up to that point, in a higher power had been virtually shattered by events I was exposed to while traveling around the world as a merchant seaman. I had experienced widely different religious beliefs and quite frankly was disenchanted with all of them. However what really prompted me to try Buddhism was the positive effect it had on my son, Craig. I, as well as others, witnessed a revolutionary change in his attitude, his behavior and his life in general.

Sincerely wanting to stop using and seeing the power manifested in his completely different outlook, I decided to try it.

I began chanting daily, as instructed, I kept the thoughts of being clean constantly in my mind. I was told that if I maintained the vision of seeing myself clean the desire to use would gradually diminish and leave completely. Each day that passed I would make a check mark on the kitchen calendar. Although the others continued using (often in my presence) yet I abstained and each day that I marked the calendar it seemed to strengthen my will to resist.

As the checks on the calendar increased so did the intensity of my chanting. I began to sense that I was in contact with the higher power that my son, Craig, and daughter, Valerie, spoke about.

The others began to notice that days were passing yet I was not using. They soon developed an admiration and respect for my abstinence. I began to feel better about myself. My self esteem began to rise. Enthusiastically I chanted more intensely than ever. I was getting stronger and knew it!

Although there was no doubt that I was getting stronger yet I did not know why. At that time I would have said that "why" was not really important. What was important was that for 120 days, four months, I used absolutely no chemical substance of any kind. This was quite an accomplishment since everyone within my immediate environment continued using!

In retrospect however, the "why" was important. If the reason had been apparent to me at the time it is likely I would not have made the serious miscalculation I did and relapsed.

Of course, it was because, through meditation, verbal affirmations, faith and strong emotion, I effectively undertook the re-programming of my subconscious mind. The positive thoughts plus the vision I constantly held of becoming clean as I chanted were the seeds that were planted and took root in my subconscious. Once there, the continuous, gradual, positive experiences influenced the subconscious and at a "definite point in time" gave rise to "something else" which was a change in attitude and behavior. What's more these changes in attitudes and behavior actually were opposite of those before. Instead of drug oriented they became non-drug oriented. And from a state of addiction arose the newly emerging state of recovery.

Looking at the check marks accumulate daily on the calendar gave me a feeling of pride. I began to really feel good about myself. My self esteem soared. Then, on the 121st day of being clean, I made a fatal miscalculation which was based on faulty judgment. I deluded myself into thinking I could control my intake of drugs by using just once. I decided to show the others and myself that I was in complete control. The others were alarmed. Why, they asked, do you want to start using again? I assured them there was no problem and I could handle it. I sincerely believed that I could. Had there been any doubt whatsoever I would never have taken that step backwards.

After the first re-introduction to my drug of choice, what do you think happened? Of course, I was unable to stop. Those twin brothers of "obsession" and "compulsion" took over, remember them? Obsession, against whom will power is no match, is why I wanted that first fix. After that it was compulsion that triggered the physical allergy that prevented me from being able to stop.

Narcotics Anonymous (N/A) sums it up in their literature this way: "One is too many and a thousand are not enough." Remember this applies only to the addict, not the mere user. The user has the will power to stop after one encounter if he so chooses. For the addict, however, there is no such choice. Once started he is powerless to stop. His only salvation lies in complete abstinence. He can never afford to take that first "hit." If he does then not only does he begin where he left off but worse yet, he starts where he would have been had he never stopped!

First I realized that my self confidence in my recovery program was really cockiness. It's positive to be confident in oneself but such confidence should be tempered with humility. This was not the case with me. I forgot that the same daily, positive, quantitative actions that led to my recovery could be radically reversed by hour to hour, negative actions. Cockiness has no place in recovery.

Second, it is fairly well admitted that drug addiction is cunning and powerful. What is not appreciated and respected is that it is also equally insidious and *patient*. More so than any other factor the characteristics of patience are lost sight of and least understood. My case was a good example. It took only 120 days of patience for my addiction to again take control. There are even better examples. There are cases where the addiction reasserted itself after years of being clean. There is no duration, the end of which time, one can safely say the danger of relapse has passed.

Third, the relapse is a time when there is an increased likelihood of an overdose. We are inclined to forget that our tolerance has diminished because of the period during which we've abstained. Unmindful of this, we often indulge to the same extent we did before and thus place our lives in peril.

These then, are some lessons I learned from my initial relapse. It could be considered a mistake but only if nothing had been learned from it. Much was learned about the nature of my addiction, the respect I must have for its awesome power and, most of all, what to do if we truly want to stay clean. I learned something else too! Something that has given me such an unshakable faith that it's only a matter of time before I'll conquer completely the addiction that has plagued my life. There are two occurrences in my past from which this faith emanates.

The first was my ability to successfully overcome the cigarette habit. I began this habit at age twelve and completely overcame it at age twenty. In my opinion nicotine is as strong as any addiction a human being could have. If one overcomes the nicotine addiction I have no doubt that he can overcome any other. Second is the above experience of my relapse.

The indisputable fact is that for 120 days I completely abstained from the use of drugs in *any* form whatsoever. What is extremely significant is that this was not accomplished under controlled circumstances, on the contrary, it was done while in the *midst* of persons who continued using on a daily and almost non-stop basis!

Though my objective to influence them by example was not realized, yet in another very important aspect I was successful.

I proved to myself that, with a strong commitment and faith in a higher power, I could overcome the desire to use. This faith and belief I have never abandoned. It was then that the realization came to me that I did not have to die an addict. That "once an addict" did not necessarily mean "always an addict."

Still something was missing. Although I'd take pride in relating to others what I had accomplished (after all, 120 days is one third of a year and while in the midst of users!) yet I did not in the least, understand the method by which such a feat was attained.

1. The Pleasure-Pain Principle

Germane to the topic of relapse is a discussion of recovery vs. abstinence as well as the pleasure-pain principle.

To abstain from the use of addictive substances differs greatly from the recovery from an addiction. Abstain is self explanatory. It is a period during which one does not use. This can be an hour, a day, a year or whatever.

Recovery is also abstinence but it is even more. It involves an active program and is concerned with establishing new values, developing new relationships and creating new interests. One who abstains from the source of his addiction without a solid basis for recovery is a very likely candidate for relapse. Indeed the best assurance that exists is for the abstaining addict to aggressively pursue a positive action plan of recovery.

The distinction between abstention and recovery is often misunderstood by many people earnestly desiring to overcome their addictions. However, it is extremely important and even critical to insulating one against the danger of relapse.

A planned program of recovery must be on a daily basis. It can take several forms. It could be making regular meetings to such places as Narcotics Anonymous or Alcoholics Anonymous. It could even be pursuing an academic program; as long as it is done on a daily basis and is geared toward the creation of new and positive relationships.

If one merely abstains from using rather than promoting a positive plan of recovery there is the likelihood of reviving old behavior patterns of action and thought. Abstention alone may lead to complacency, overconfidence and cockiness. Along with this is the somewhat seductive nature of the practical environment. This, in essence, is forced abstention. A good example of this is the confinement in jails and other institutions. When thus removed from the object of our addictions we become readily lulled into a state of complacency. We erroneously think all is well. It is easily forgotten that the powerful and destructive obsession is still lurking within our subconscious. It is ready at any given opportunity to reassert itself and again take control of our lives. We have willed never to use again but fail to realize that will power is no match for obsession.

Recovery is the top priority in our lives. This means that staying clean should always be above all else. If this is kept in mind, relapse, partial or total, will at best be only temporary. Once we accept accountability for our recovery and shed guilt for being addicted, we are making an important step toward changing our lives. It is beyond contradiction (or should be) that *we are not criminals* but rather emotionally, mentally, and spiritually as well as physically ill individuals.

In this overall context pleasure and pain are two emotional experiences that are worthy of consideration. They are especially central to any understanding of how to stay clean.

Whatever reason that's given for using mind altering substances by far the most common is, "I like the way it makes me feel" and "It's pleasurable."

It is as if there is pain when we want to indulge yet can't find a "reward" when finally we're able to do so. This brings to mind what a friend often said, "Somewhere I read in a book, things aren't always the way they look."

This statement could certainly be applied here because the situation is actually the opposite of what is usually thought.

What seems at first to be pleasure is, in the final analysis, pain; and what we think we feel as pain is, in the long run, actually pleasure. The pain we feel when denied access to the object of our addiction, is really only a temporary sacrifice. A fleeting sacrifice for the ultimate pleasure that comes from being clean and serene! The pleasure derived from using, since it's only temporary, is illusory and without substance. We overlook the fact that a few hours or less of mental discomfort will pass. Such a transitory uneasiness is much to be preferred over the years of emotional and spiritual pain that will inevitably follow using again.

The thought of that first fix blinds us to the insanity of our action. N/A and A/A gives us the classic definition of insanity. "It is", they say, "repeating the same action and expecting different results."

We don't realize that it's the pursuit of so called pleasure that invariably gets us into trouble. Most of our problems surface when we are indulging in these so called "pleasures."

Problems, especially of a legal nature, never arise when we sincerely deal with the "pain" that comes from abstinence. Furthermore what we consider as pain that comes from not using is really a "reward." It results in a genuine pleasure that we experience in a renewed high self esteem; a feeling good about ourselves.

2. *Decisions*

One day we'll certainly have to say
To ourselves "This is enough"

It makes no sense to continue to pay
But to quit will be real tough

It's nice to freak and have a blast
Seems like you're floating in the sky

What's cold is it doesn't last
Like the natural ways of getting high

For there is no feeling like feeling good
It takes no chemical to feel this way

Who'd want to beat it even if you could?
Especially when you don't have to pay

It's natural and free, and this is the key
To avoiding that constant yearn

The highs are plenty, yet cost not a penny
And unlike a chemical, there's no need to
Return

I truly believe that there is no high like "feeling good." What's more, it's free!

I also believe that once you partake of any drug (and like it) it's a distinct possibility at that precise moment you may be psychologically addicted.

A common mistake made when a relapse is imminent is thinking about the pleasure we received rather than the pain we will have to endure. If these two experiences were objectively weighed it would be clear as to what path we should choose. The immediate pleasure is at best short lived; the pain is nothing short of a "reward" and results in pleasure and happiness afterwards.

If we thought more of the negative experiences, the overdoses, the downright frightening events we have experienced in connection with our addictions then it would be less difficult to take affirmative action to overcome them. One thing is certain, we would be far less likely to relapse once a positive program of recovery was undertaken. Unfortunately the fleeting pleasure from that initial fix is what we think about the most. It's only after we have relapsed that reality sets in and we began to think about all of the negative consequences of our action. Then it's too late and we begin to suffer from feelings of despair, hopelessness, self pity and a general loss of self esteem.

As a result of extended depression we feel at a loss to understand our action. We ask ourselves, "Why did I do it, when I was doing so well?" "I had no intention of doing it. It occurred before I knew it. Evidently I'm destined to die an addict; maybe I'd be better off if I did."

These are the type of thoughts that go through our head when we relapse. At this point these thoughts are to be expected and to be alarmed by them is to miss the point.

The point is to educate people to the decisive role of the subconscious mind in preventing relapse.

We must begin to appreciate the truth that if we are clean we are successful. This is the most important thing in our lives and is the one and *only* yardstick by which success is measured. This is the base that supports the entire superstructure of our lives. Whatever our material accomplishments are, if we are not clean we are failures. We are failures mentally, emotionally and above all we are failures spiritually.

Of course whether or not we are becoming non addicts is a matter that's entirely up to us. It's a choice we must make for ourselves. Do we strongly desire to overcome our addiction? Once we stop using do we really want to stay clean?

Arriving at this decision is perhaps the major stumbling block to undertaking a program of recovery. Underlining this decision is the belief that what happened to clean addicts can also happen to us if we really want it to. The sad fact however, is that most who profess a desire for change do not truly wish to do so. Once the resolve exists to turn our lives around the road ahead still remains difficult. However, without a firm determination it is virtually impossible. Then again we may think we want to change but truly don't. Our actions often belie what we want to do.

It's safe to say that over half of those who suffer relapse fall into this category. Oftentimes they are unaware of the contradiction between their conscious and subconscious mind, between what they think and what they do. As we know the conscious and subconscious have separate and distinct functions. If there is such a contradiction then the seeds of desire were not effectively planted in the subconscious garden. The thought may have been consciously entertained but it was a fleeting one, not rooted in faith or strong emotional and spiritual commitment.

There is an irony that exists here as regards those considered weak as opposed to the "so called" strong. The weak, believe it or not, are the first, usually, to undertake a program of recovery. The strong are often the last. This probably seems strange to you and a good question would be, "Why is this so", if indeed it is. Well it is, and the reason is because the "weak" are usually the ones who are non-functional. Their weakness prevents them from discharging even basic responsibilities and therefore they very soon realize they are "powerless" over their addiction and their lives have truly become "unmanageable." They seek help readily.

On the other hand the so called strong are the ones who remain within the grasp of addiction longer mainly because (1) they are *not* non-functional. They are able to perform on a daily basis (although at reduced efficiency) and (2) they are usually in a state of denial; making excuses and blaming others for their problems. Consequently, they are the ones who must hit rock bottom before realization sets in as to their "powerlessness" and the "unmanageability" of their lives.

Once the decision is made to turn our lives around; a decision by the way that must be spiritual; we must view our addiction in terms of its origin and progression. We must understand that we weren't always addicted. Therefore, retrospectively, we should determine the circumstances surrounding the birth of our addiction as well as those that contributed to its growth and development.

Here again it's important to keep in mind the quantitative character of these circumstances. We know from previous discussion that our addiction was born mainly from our environmental circumstances. Their repetitive, continuous influence was thus quantitative in nature and gave rise to something different. This qualitatively different something was, of course, our state of addiction.

Further in tracing these circumstances, we are able to see that they were negative in nature. They remained basically drug oriented up to the point at which we made a spiritual commitment to change direction of our lives.

By such retrospective thinking, by going back to the origin of our addiction, and following its development, we have a sound notion as to who we are and where we are. We certainly know that we are the opposite of what we were before and also of what we want to become.

What's so important in such an analysis is that by doing so we get a grip on the external driving force of change; the environmental circumstances. It's a confirmation of the fact that each of us is the sum total of our experiences. A confirmation of the universal law of quantity and quality.

Once the relapse occurs it's not the end of the world. While basically a negative experience, it's not without positive aspects. Nothing is. Indeed for some it is the necessary catalyst that causes them to truly awaken to the danger of addiction. It can be the second chance they need. The big gamble is; will you survive the relapse? Unfortunately for some there is no second chance; they will die.

Prevention is still the best course to take. Many signs are apparent before an impending relapse becomes a reality.

One sign is a negative attitude. On the ladder of recovery remember that attitude determines altitude. What is the right altitude? It's the one you have when the spiritual principles are incorporated in your daily life. They are attitudes of love, honesty, acceptance, sharing and humility. The negative attitudes are the opposite of those. They are arrogance, self centeredness, dishonesty, self pity, resentment, to name a few.

When these latter attitudes begin to creep into our consciousness they become the emotional and spiritual precursors to physical relapse. It's often necessary for us to relearn positive things in order to combat the many negatives that will always strive to reassert themselves.

We should never isolate ourselves if we are to prevent a relapse. It is said that an "addict alone is in bad company." It's highly improbable to develop attitudes of spirituality when we are alone. This is the main advantage group therapy holds over individual effort. Interaction with others facilitates a positive development. It then becomes easy for us to share, tolerate, accept, love, be humble and unselfish. In other words it is easy for us to become spiritual.

Remember not to be afraid of the feelings to use. The urges will come. However just as they come they will surely pass. Don't try to control your use. It is wishful thinking to believe you can use in moderation. It won't work because you're addicted and the twin brothers of obsession and compulsion will assure that it won't work. Remember too that the immediate gratification is not worth the long time misery. The relapse subjects you to added dangers. Your tolerance has been reduced by being clean and you're therefore more vulnerable to overdose than ever before. Your normal intake before relapse could now be fatal. If you're fortunate to survive a relapse get back to a group meeting as soon as possible.

Spirituality

We recently touched upon a few of the spiritual principles. Others are open-mindedness, gratitude, empathy, forgiveness and patience.

Many suffering from addiction make the mistake of equating spirituality with religion. This is the most common barrier against recovery. It is a misconception that was an obstacle to my acceptance of the Narcotics Anonymous program before I understood their program was not religious but spiritual.

The "higher power" concept of both N/A and A/A explicitly states it is the "God of *your* understanding" as it relates to each individual. In other words whatever higher power concept with which you might be comfortable is the one for you. There are no mystical or religious connotations to it and your higher power could very well be the "group" or whatever. This enables many to embrace their programs who, in good conscious, would be otherwise unable to do so.

Solution 1

Something you should know, when you're low
Especially if you're hooked on dope

Whatever the extent, this formula is meant
To give you more than just hope

The mighty power, governing us every hour
Is that on which you must call

However deep your problems, you can solve them
It matters not how hard you fall

It's your subconscious mind, when you appear blind
That enables you to see

Think you can't stop, and get back on top
Then take this advice from me

Study the subconscious mind, you'll surely find
This is the seat of your habit

Before you do, it's usually true
You must say to yourself, I've had it

Whatever your quirks, when asked if it works
It gives an affirmative nod

Regardless of the name, it's still the same
Whether it's called *mind, nature* or *God!*

These programs merely take into account what has been recognized by man from time immemorial. That is simply that some "force" governs the regularity of the universe. We see it daily in the passing of day into night and one season into another.

The God of your understanding concept leaves it up to each individual to select that with which he may be most comfortable to him. It is very broad in its application.

Spiritual development tends to promote successful recovery. This is so precisely because the attitude of the addict is directly opposite to the spiritual principles previously mentioned. Instead of dishonesty there is honesty, selfishness gives rise to unselfishness; intolerance is replaced by tolerance; acceptance instead of resentment and humility for arrogance. When these attitudes begin to change into their opposites, the addict also changes into his. He changes from a non spiritual to a spiritual person.

It is important as previously pointed out to recognize that isolation does not tend to promote spiritual growth. It is not easy to grow spiritually when we are alone (although we are really never alone, even in isolation). For that reason all successful treatment programs stress the importance of the "group." Sharing your experiences with others persons with a similar problem is extremely effective in insuring continued recovery. When we are isolated with our disease it progresses to the point which we made a spiritual commitment to change direction of our lives.

By such retrospective thinking, by going back to the origin of our addiction, and following its development, we have a sound notion as to who we are and where we are. We certainly know that we are the opposite of what we were before and also of what we want to become.

What's so important in such an analysis is that by doing so we get a grip on the external driving force of change; the environmental circumstances. It's a confirmation of the fact that each of us is the sum total of our experiences. A confirmation of the universal law of quantity and quality.

Once the relapse occurs it's not the end of the world. While basically a negative experience, it's not without positive aspects. Nothing is. Indeed for some it is the necessary catalyst that causes them to truly awaken to the danger of addiction. It can be the second chance they need. The big gamble is; will you survive the relapse? Unfortunately for some there is no second chance; they die.

Prevention is still the best course to take. Many signs are apparent before an impending relapse becomes a reality.

One sign is a negative attitude. On the ladder of recovery remember that attitude determines altitude. What is the right attitude? It's the one you have when the spiritual principles are incorporated in your daily life. They are attitudes of love, honesty, acceptance, sharing, and humility. The negative attitudes are the opposite of those. They are arrogance, self centeredness, dishonesty, self pity, resentment, to name a few.

When these latter attitudes begin to creep into our consciousness they become the emotional and spiritual precursors to physical relapse. It's often necessary for us to relearn positive things in order to combat the many negatives that will always strive to reassert themselves.

We should never isolate ourselves if we are to prevent a relapse. It is said that an "addict alone is in bad company." It's highly improbable to develop attitudes of spirituality when we are alone. This is the main advantage group therapy holds over individual effort. Interaction with others facilitates a positive development. It then becomes easy for us to share, tolerate, accept, love, be humble and unselfish. In other words it is easy for us to become spiritual.

Remember not to be afraid of the feelings to use. The urges will come. However just as they come they will surely pass. Don't try to control your use. It is wishful thinking to believe you can use in moderation. It won't work because you're addicted and the twin brothers of obsession and compulsion will assure that it won't work. Remember too that the immediate gratification is not worth the long time misery. The relapse subjects you to added dangers. Your tolerance has been reduced by being clean and you're therefore more vulnerable to overdose than ever.

The Twelve Step Program

There is no doubt whatsoever that the programs of Alcoholics Anonymous and Narcotics Anonymous work. A/A was the forerunner of N/A and the latter developed its twelve step program from the former. The program of N/A actually expanded the A/A program beyond a single substance and included addiction as a whole. The experiences of both programs in successfully rehabilitating thousands of addicts are nationally and internationally known and respected. Their ultimate goals are the same; re-programming of the subconscious mind. However this is not an openly avowed goal in either program. I truly believe they should make every recovering addict aware of this omission, nevertheless their programs work because they are based on spiritual principles and are therefore extremely practical.

I shall attempt to show how these two programs work as far as developing and maintaining the spiritual principles that are essential to an effective recovery.

How this is done in N/A is ironically by the acronym H.O.W. This represents the three basic principles necessary in order to begin the recovery process.

(H) stands for honesty. Experience shows that there is no such thing as an honest addict. All addicts are dishonest. It therefore follows that developing a condition of honesty would have the effect of transforming an addict into something other than an addict; a non addict. This is also one of the most difficult and challenging steps to take. It is also one of the most basic. Until the addict truly gets honest (with himself in particular) any meaningful rehabilitation or recovery from the throes of his addiction is impossible.

It makes no difference how much he knows or what amount of theory he has. The bottom line is not what he knows or what his theory is; rather what he does, what practical results he obtains.

Some think they are honest when in reality they have at best an illusion of honesty. This was my situation.

After my first manuscript was accepted for publication it was natural for me to assume I knew how to proceed to a successful recovery. I had enough theory but what I lacked was the correct practice. What's more I thought I was being honest with myself. The illusion of honesty, however, can last only so long. Eventually reality sets in. So it was with me. I had to come to grasp with my rationalizations. My "playmates", "play-toys" and "playthings" were not new. They were a cut from the same old mold. My environment began to control me instead of me exercising control over it. My addiction began to reassert itself. I realized that the disease of addiction is not only "cunning" and "powerful" but "patient" as well. This patience is often lost sight of and after a period of time we lapse into a state of complacency.

Honesty takes courage and both are necessary in working the first step of the twelve step program.

The first step says "we admitted we were powerless over our addiction, that our lives had become unmanageable."

In order to make such an admission we must not only display the spiritual principle of honesty but also humility and courage. These are spiritual principles that can not permanently reside in the consciousness of the addict. With the addict it is dishonesty, arrogance and cowardice. Furthermore the admission of being powerless is merely the first half of the first step.

The second half requires acceptance of the fact that our life has become "unmanageable." Here again the addict is faced with the spiritual principle of "acceptance." Also here acceptance must be cultivated because it is not present in the subconscious garden or the addict's mind. Instead the seeds of anger and resentment have been planted.

Working this first step inevitably produces a positive change in the attitude of the addict. The door is now open and he is ready to cross the threshold into recovery.

The second step asks us to "believe in a power greater than ourselves" who "could restore us to sanity." This requires open mindedness and is the (O) of the acronym H.O.W. The addict may give lip service to belief in such a power but more often than not in practice it's just the opposite. He certainly would resent being called insane but yet he continually "repeats the same action and doesn't realize the results must be the same." This is insanity. It ignores the universal law of cause and effect.

The next attitude necessary for spiritual rejuvenation is embodied in the third step of the twelve step program. It is the (W) and means there must be a "willingness" and a "decision" on the part of the one seeking recovery to "turn our will and our lives over to the care of God as we understand him."

Many seeking recovery had a problem with the traditional "God" concept. Being a practicing Buddhist it presented (what I thought was) a major barrier to my own acceptance of the N/A program until I realized that it was not the traditional religious concept that was in issue but rather the acceptance of a "force" greater than I. This higher power had a very broad interpretation and could, for all practical purposes, even include the N/A group as a whole. For the truth of the matter is, in actual practice, it is a "force" greater than any individual. This is so because it represents the combined wisdom and experience of those suffering from a common problem. It is not difficult to surrender to the "will" of the "group" once it is realized that it indeed is a "higher power."

This, then, constitutes the H.O.W., (the how to get started) of two of the most successful recovery programs ever undertaken. Once honesty, open mindedness and willingness have been displayed by the addict, he is well on his way to recovery. These are the three most important and basic spiritual principles, and I experienced the exhilaration that comes from practicing them, the result was an experience of not only being clean but also being serene. Few realize that it's possible to be clean yet not be serene. Serenity comes from actively working the twelve steps.

In my first book, *"Crack, You and Your Loved Ones"*, I presented a method which, when put to the test, will enable one to stop using. However, as previously pointed out, becoming clean and remaining clean are two entirely different processes. Besides one can actually attain a state of being clean yet not have that all important "peace of mind." This is what prompted me to devote additional effort to write a sequel to my first manuscript. I came to the conclusion that one will eventually use again without actively working the twelve step program or a reasonable facsimile.

I have never heard of or seen an evidence of a person relapsing who assiduously and faithfully practices the principles of this program. For that reason, more than any other, it is appropriate at this point, to continue the discussion and interpretation of these important steps.

Our discussion ended with the third step. The first three steps are merely the necessary prerequisites for successfully practicing the remaining nine.

Now we will proceed to the all important fourth step. This tells us to "make a searching and fearless moral inventory of ourselves."

Without a doubt this is the most challenging step of all. This is so mainly because the mere presence of the words "searching" and "fearless" give rise to feelings of reluctance, apprehension and downright fear. We find all kinds of excuses to postpone writing down our defects of character and other liabilities which we know we have yet want to keep from coming to the surface.

We fail to realize that everyone has his skeletons in the closet. Further, this is not merely an unmasking of our faults and defects but of our assets as well.

It is an inventory of our past and is designed to let us know ourselves and exactly where we are. Once this is known we can then discard the negative and retain the positive. It is important to a proper perspective for one to have knowledge of both one's liabilities as well as assets.

There is no question that such a self evaluation takes courage, however the rewards are great. Stress is released and our subconscious rewards us with a true state of serenity plus a strong desire to stay clean.

Serenity is extremely important because it removes the likelihood of relapse. As previously mentioned, being clean does not necessarily mean being serene. It's entirely possible to be clean yet have a troubled mind. Diligent practice of the twelve step program is the assurance that one will be serene as well as clean.

This must be viewed as an ongoing endeavor and not a one time event. As new problems arise one must apply the steps to them. Writing about them as they arise has the effect of eliminating stress. Thus we are able to maintain a state of tranquility.

It is well to keep it mind that the steps be worked in sequence in the first undertaking. Step two should not be started without completing step one and so forth. However, after finishing step twelve one could return and rework any particular step.

In step five it says "we admitted to our 'higher power' to ourselves and to another the exact nature of our wrongs." Key words here are "higher power" and "another human being."

As we fore stated "higher power" is broad in its interpretation and can encompass any belief from the traditional religious concept to the acceptance of the "support group."

"Another human being" is usually the one chosen to be your sponsor although it doesn't have to be. It could be anyone. There must however be trust in them. They must also understand exactly what you are trying to accomplish and your reason for doing so.

Admitting "to ourselves" may first seem to be a repeat of step four but it isn't. Step four pin-points the problem and begins the solution. Step five goes further and actually continues the process begun by sharing it "with another human being." Important feedback is obtained by taking this objective step. Compassion as well as understanding can be a positive factor here. This is often reflected in the "other human being" recounting similar experiences of his own. For that reason it is very beneficial to choose a person with a similar problem.

It can be seen that the main difference between step four and step five is that the former concerns itself merely with writing whereas the latter involves not only writing but also sharing that which is written. In step four we made a thorough and detailed inventory but in step five we actively deal with the subject matter of that inventory, it is not sufficient to merely write about the past. We must share with "another person" the "exact nature" of our past wrongs. This means that, instead of being nebulous and vague, we must be clear, specific and unambiguous with regard to the subject matter we share.

It will be known when the need arises to work the steps because our serenity will be disturbed. Likewise it will be known when we have successfully worked the steps because then our feelings of spirituality will be enhanced.

Step six says "we were entirely ready to have God (of our understanding) remove all these defects of character."

Here the operative words are "entirely ready" and "remove." Willingness is central here too. It was first referred to in step three and was stated as a "requirement." Here it assumes different proportions. Willingness here also means complete readiness to have our "higher power" remove our defects. Having written about our defects and assets and having shared them with "another person" we now, with humility, surrender our will to that of our "higher power." Now from our new found spirituality springs forth hope and anticipation of a new life.

Humility leads us into step seven and it is the natural consequences of the honesty which, at this point, is becoming part of our lives. Step seven tells us "to humbly ask our higher power to remove our shortcomings."

If arrogance is essential to being addicted, humility is indispensable to being clean, for as we have seen, whatever is true for the state of addiction, the opposite is true for the state of recovery.

We realize now that we don't have all of the answers. If we are in a negative, unproductive state as a result of our addiction we must accept the fact that "our best thinking got us into the mess we are in." To extricate ourselves we know we must submit to the wisdom of our higher power. As we said oftentimes this is our "support group" with its collective experience of thousands of successful recovering addicts.

The decision has been made. We now generously desire the destructive traits to be removed from our character. We are honest. We have fully accepted the fact that we are powerless and out of control. We are slaves to the awesome powers of obsession and compulsion. The former repeatedly takes us back to that to which we are addicted while the latter triggers the reinforcement action that prevents us from stopping once we have started.

We have surrendered our will to our higher power; took an inventory of our assts as well as our liabilities; shared them with another human being and now are completely ready and willing to have our shortcomings removed. In step eight "we made a list of all persons we had harmed and became willing to make amends to them."

Here, usually, the inventory list of step four again comes into play. To it, however, is added those whom we have not only harmed but also wronged. Between harmed and wronged there is a distinction which, while slight, yet should be noted. One can conceivably be wronged and not necessarily be harmed. Harm carries with it some form of "hurt" usually resulting from "lies", "broken promises" or more directly "inflicting pain." It can range from mental discomfort to outright physical pain. However, one can be "wronged" merely through injustice.

This is what we deal with in step eight, the injustice which, in one way or another, we have bestowed upon someone else. These are the people who should be added to our list. It should be noted that we do it through someone else. Direct confrontation may not be the wisest course to take. Other times it could be a situation where we are just unable to locate the person. In such a case it will be sufficient if we are merely but truly willing to contact them. If we attempt to make amends and are unable to do so we can still take the comfort in maintaining our serenity just by staying clean. It will help to keep in mind that we have a selfish motive. Not only do we seek to be forgiven but we also seek peace of mind and the evaluation of our self esteem.

Although there should not be undue delay in implementing this step yet there should be patience. There may exist delicate circumstances, nevertheless this step must be completed. Step ten says, "We continued to take personal inventory and when we were wrong promptly admitted it."

This step is vital for an ongoing evaluation of ourselves and in particular our attitudes, reactions and relationships. We must keep abreast of our defects and shortcomings and here we are given the tool for constant vigilance.

Our old ways of thinking are always capable of reasserting themselves but by practicing this step we are able to prevent their recurrence. It is thus a good check to see if we are headed for possible relapse.

Living without drugs for us is abnormal during recovery. We often become angry and resentful and such anger and resentment must be sought out and dealt with if we are able to continue progress. This, together with the loneliness we often experience, causes us problems.

This step too must be worked constantly. It is basically a step of prevention and our aim is to prevent trouble before it arises. We must be real and not make excuses for our actions but maintain vigilance constantly. We must watch our emotions as well as our actions and not be fooled by false feelings of serenity.

Recovery is our responsibility. An ongoing inventory frees us from our past and prepares us for our future. It is the essence of responsibility.

It is in step eleven, in my opinion, that the subconscious mind, with its awesome spiritual power, should be dealt with; it should dominate any discussion involving contact with "God of our understanding."

Step eleven as stated by the official text of Narcotics Anonymous says, "We sought through prayer and meditation to improve our conscious contact with God as we understood him, praying only for knowledge of his will for us and the power to carry that out."

Here the concern is with prayer and meditation. It is emphasized "that we have a system of belief that works for us." It is not essential to our acceptance of either Narcotics Anonymous or Alcoholics Anonymous that we subscribe to any particular religion or any specific belief but merely one that "works for us." The "God of our understanding" so to speak. The bottom line in recovery, they teach, is not what or in whom you believe, but rather the results obtained when recovery is undertaken.

Permit me to extract another quote from the official text of Narcotics Anonymous.

"Sometimes when we pray, a remarkable thing happens. We find the ways, means and energies to perform tasks far beyond our capacities. We grasp the limitless strength provided to us through our daily prayer and surrender, as long as we keep faith and renew it." And further, "for those who do not pray, meditation is our only way of working this step. A basic premise of meditation is that it is difficult, if not impossible, to obtain conscious contact with our higher power unless our mind is still."

The preceding quote indicates this is precisely the step where, I believe, the inseparable connection between our subconscious and spirituality on the one hand and our higher power on the other, should be thoroughly understood.

Toward that end I shall employ the method of first extracting a quote from the eleventh step as stated in the official text of Narcotics Anonymous after which it will be commented upon in terms of its relation to the subconscious mind. It says:

"The nature of our belief will determine the manner of our prayers and meditations. We need only to make sure that we have a system of belief that works for us. Results count in recovery."

From the quote the inference to be drawn is that once we come to believe in the power of the subconscious the "manner of meditation" will take the form of verbal affirmations. This individual effort, this consciously planting of the seeds of drug free thoughts in our subconscious will eventually grow into drug free attitudes and drug free behavior, why? Because like the gardener who plants his seeds, we reap what we sow!

Another statement says "the purpose of the eleventh step is to increase our awareness of that power."

If this is its purpose it can thus be no contradiction in any attempt to bring into focus the spiritual power of the subconscious and its connection to the universal higher power.

A third quote, "we usually feel something is different in the moment but don't see the change in our lives until later."

This is truly consistent with how the subconscious mind works. The thoughts received by it from the conscious mind are acted upon in silence and, like the seeds planted in a garden, we don't see the change until later; until they sprout from the surface of the soil.

The next quote breaks away from the traditional religious concept. It says:

"Outside of Narcotics Anonymous, there are a number of different groups practicing meditation. Nearly all these groups are connected with a particular religion or philosophy. An endorsement of anyone of these methods would be a violation of our traditions and a restriction on the individual right to have a "God of his understanding." *Meditation allows us to develop spirituality in our own way.*

Here the removal of the philosophy of Narcotics Anonymous from the narrow confines of traditional religious concepts and broadening it to include an individual's right to a "God of his understanding, is to be applauded." Meditation allows us to develop spirituality in our own way. Therefore the concept of the subconscious with its effect on our attitudes, habits and behavior should be subjected to the infallible test of practice.

The brackets inserted in the following quote are mine. "Prayer [meditation] is communicating our concerns to a power greater than ourselves. Sometimes when we pray [meditate] a remarkable thing happens. We find the way, means and energies to perform tasks far beyond our capacities. We grasp the limitless strength provided for us through our daily prayer [meditation] and surrender, as long as we keep faith and renew it. It's easy to float back out the door on a cloud of religious zeal and forget that we are addicts with an incurable disease. For those who do not pray, meditation is the only way of working this step."

This tells us that a reprogramming of the subconscious through individual meditation is not inconsistent with the philosophy of Narcotics Anonymous and that practical results that follow are often "far beyond our capacities."

Further confirmation is found in the following quote; "Quieting the mind through meditation brings us inner peace that brings us into contact with the God within us. Through constant contact with our higher power, the answers we seek come to us."

How consistent this is with how I feel the subconscious should be viewed! It is through it that we contact that part of the higher power that's in each of us. Acknowledging that, "the kingdom of God is with you" gives powerful weight to an important assertion. It's the assertion that programming the subconscious either individually or by group treatment is effective in establishing spiritual principles conducive to recovery.

The final quote says, "There is a spiritual principle of giving away what we have in order to keep it."

When I first heard in Narcotics Anonymous meetings that "we keep what we have by giving it away", I did not understand what was meant but such a statement. It really became clear after I began, on my own, to reprogram my subconscious mind. I began to see the connection between it and the concept of the "God of my understanding." I began to think about the benefit those who were reluctant to enter treatment programs could gain by this knowledge.

I thought about ways to get people to grasp a tool which they could use on their own and which was yet based on the unfailing principles of

Narcotics Anonymous and Alcoholics Anonymous. Principles and practices proven by the experience of hundreds of thousands of clean addicts.

It was later when learning of the relation between the subconscious and conscious mind that I realized this was something I really wanted to keep. But the only way to keep it was to "give it away." Thus I began to promote a general awareness, especially among those addicted, of how our addictions could be overcome by reprogramming the subconscious. Indeed, there is really no other way it can be done! Mostly it is accomplished without the knowledge of the one addicted. It is my contention that if there were awareness on the part of the one involved, he or she could individually exert some added influence by using the unique "selective" power of the conscious mind in the reprogramming process.

Having said that we now turn to the final step in the twelve step program.

Step twelve says, "Having had a spiritual awakening as a result of these [previous] steps, we tried to carry this message to addicts, and to practice these principles in all of our affairs."

The principle of "keeping what we have by giving it away" reaches its peak here. The emphasis is upon carrying the message to all who "want it." There are many now who "need it" but they are not the focus of our effort because in many instances it would be a fatal effort. We must concentrate on those who truly "want" a new life. That's why the doors of most treatment programs are locked, not from the inside but from the outside. No one is kept against his will.

It is continually pointed out that the program works, however the most effective method is to spread the message not by words but by example. An addict is in the unique position of being able to help another addict more than anyone else. This is so because of more or less similar experiences. This is also the value of group meetings. However different one may think his or her situation is yet sooner or later someone, at a meeting, will share an experience parallel to his. This is when the benefit comes. Also there is benefit to the one actually sharing. It is an important reinforcement against probability of relapse.

This concludes the twelve steps which are the core of two of the most successful treatment programs ever undertaken.

There is no recorded testimony of a single instance involving the relapse of one who faithfully and consistently practiced these steps.

It is important to point out that it is an ongoing plan which should be repeated as new problems arise in one's life. Addictions are arrested. They are never cured. However, with an effective ongoing plan of recovery and a positive support system, the addiction can be arrested for a lifetime. We never need to use again.

This freedom to have a new life was something not always available to one suffering from the disease of addiction. There was a time when the phrase "an addict for life" carried with it a hopelessness since there is no cure. Now however that view is not unconditionally accepted, the distinction must be drawn again between the using as opposed to the non-using addict. They are not the same. The non-using addict is, for practical purposes, in a state of recovery.

The successful theories evolved from a practical need and withstood the test of practice in order to establish themselves no longer as mere theories but truths. There is no argument with success.

It is also said that "an addict alone is in bad company." The basis for such a statement was the obvious benefit to be derived from support obtained during recovery. There is no question that such a situation is preferred to that of dealing with the problem outside of a group. There is so much to be gained from sharing the testimony of those with similar experiences.

However, this is not to say that the addict is "alone" outside of the group. He may appear to be isolated buy in reality he is not. Quite frankly, he is never completely alone, never completely isolated. Even when undertaking on his own to reprogram the subconscious by verbal affirmations; even when retreating into his own solitude, his higher power is with him.

In fact, it's a law of the universe, as we learned, that nothing exists in isolation. Things and phenomena are never apart from the circumstances of existence. So it is with an individual addict. This is another reason why it's so important for one addicted to know that, while treatment programs are ideal means to deal with addiction, still there are positive steps to be taken on one's own.

Through conscious thought selection the seeds of recovery can be individually planted in the garden of the subconscious mind. Spiritual contact can also be established with the higher power. One is never alone if faith exists in the "God of *your* understanding."

The road to recovery can begin by understanding an individual program of meditation but later on there exists a void which is nonexistent in the group program. This void is filled, in a group program, by new relationships, new activities and new interests. Without establishing these new habit patterns the void will be filled by an eventual return of the old relationships, old activities and old interests.

1. *Becoming*

> Got off the track? Don't look back
> The past has come and gone
>
> The bad you leave, the good you retrieve
> And then you get right back on
>
> Don't shed tears, for what is
> What's more important instead
>
> Is that you see, what you *will* be
> Which means you look ahead
>
> What was before, is no more
> That's all in the past
>
> And what is now, will change somehow
> Even the present doesn't last
>
> This is the key, believe you me
> As you stroll along life's path humming
>
> All the world you'll show, you really know
> What's important is *what's becoming*!

Everything that exists, at one time did not exist at all and every existing entity will inevitably pass away. We can't be shackled even by the present because it too is passing away before our very eyes! What we can and must do, through our actions, attitude and behavior, is to shape our future. By means of our conscious power of selection it can take a positive shape. On the other hand it may assume a negative character. While it is impossible to thwart change yet we do have a choice. We must ensure that for the future, it will be positive. Thus we can, through a subjective, positive reprogramming of our subconscious effectively determine our own destiny!

We need not bemoan the notion that as a result of our addiction things are hopeless for us: that we are addicts and "once an addict, always an addict." Now we see the picture clearer than ever before. As a result of our new way of thinking, of grasping the world as it really is, we accept our addiction in an entirely different light.

Now we see ourselves not only as what we are (addicts) but more importantly what we are becoming (recovering non-addicts).

What's significant about our ability to consciously select our thoughts and relationships is that we can assure that what is *becoming* in our lives will be positive and to our benefit instead of negative and to our detriment.

In either case the quantitative circumstances are going to give rise to a certain qualitative entity. The law is equally applicable. Our conscious selection is *only* determinative of the direction of change, whether it will be positive or negative. There is no other power of force that can permanently impede its movement.

Lest we forget, the law is that a certain amount of something applied to something, at a definite point in time, gives rise to something else; and that something else is different and usually the opposite of "what was before."

If we choose to persist in the same environmental experiences that ushered in and maintained our addiction then we will remain addicted (and get progressively worse) because such experiences are of a negative drug oriented nature. On the other hand if we strongly commit ourselves to overcoming our addiction we will inevitably make the positive choice. We will choose to embark on a program of recovery. We will seek new relationships, and new interests. By an understanding of the scientific laws of universal change and development and the application of them in our daily struggle to redirect our lives, we will ultimately prevail.

This is not to say there will not be setbacks and disappointments. Change and development are seldom smooth. There likely will be relapse of partial or even total nature. However even so we should not be dissuaded. We should be unwavering in our resolve to succeed. We must bear in mind that the struggle is like war and to be victorious in war oftentimes we must temporarily retreat in order to advance.

If we waiver or give in to our disease we are doomed. Drug addiction is progressive and fatal. If we are lucky we are arrested and go to jail or prison. Lucky because then by merely getting arrested we are actually rescued, inasmuch as we have another chance at living.

We may feel, after incarceration, that all is lost. It's natural to feel that way but it's beneficial to stop and ponder the question, "What am I really living for? What is the purpose of life?"

When we seriously ask ourselves this question there is really only one answer that makes sense. The purpose of living, in the final analysis, is to be happy. Not material possessions; not positions of power; not money, but happiness is the life condition towards which everyone consciously or unconsciously aspires.

Accepting this as basically true then our first priority as those suffering from addiction, should be to stay clean. Without this state of being, any claim to happiness is an illusion.

When we first began using we did it in order to feel good. Then we did it so that we would feel different. Later the luster was lost and we really didn't know why we did it.

Those of us who took honest inventory of ourselves were led to an admission of our powerlessness over our addiction and the acceptance of the wretched condition of our lives.

Some of us hit bottom and were forced to seek help. Others continued to try and "dodge the bullet" by resorting to all kinds of lies, deceit and manipulations which is the stock in trade of addicts. Inevitably came the jails, hospitals and prisons. Those of us who were honest enough to admit it knew that these institutions were actually a blessing in disguise. We were driven to the conclusions that, while they were basically negative experiences yet there was also a very strong positive element.

We realized that in a very real sense we were rescued instead of arrested. That the apparent heart attacks we had which resulted in our being hospitalized were not heart attacks but the result of coronary vaso-spasms. This condition reverses itself once cocaine usage stops.

Also we discovered that the meetings we attended in prison brought us a serenity and, if you will, a happiness that we never experienced while using. We begin to share our experiences with other inmates who had similar problems.

The bottom line was that we knew we had a second chance to make something positive out of our lives and we were grateful. We talked with each other about the utter stupidity of using drugs; how they had robbed us of our health, finances, self esteem, and rendered us spiritually bankrupt. We made lists of the pros and cons of using and saw that the cons far outweighed the pros. We made elaborate plans to take a different route upon our release. Underneath it all, we were happy.

Word reached us from the outside as to the status of those we knew who were still using. None of the communications was rosy. They were either "looking bad", "losing weight" or "tripping" and "freaking out." There were ongoing accounts of violence among the dealers involving what turf belonged to whom. They constantly looked over their shoulders and viewed everyone with suspicion.

When the inevitable arrests came and they entered jail their focus seemed to reflect relief as preparations were made for their adjustment to the controlled environment.

It's as if they were saying, "I've been unable to do it now you manage my life for me. Help me to get my house in order and prepare me for a second chance. I am much better off now than I was on the outside. Out there it is a one way street that leads to a dead end!"

It's as if they have willingly and peacefully resigned themselves to the radical alteration of their lifestyle. In a sense they have finally entered a treatment program. The principle difference being that this one is involuntary and against their conscious will.

Note that I said their "conscious" will. I say this because I truly believe their subconscious minds actually "willed" that they get themselves arrested. Indeed if it is true that, in the final analysis, the subconscious is the regulator of our attitudes and behavior, then it is certainly conceivable that the subconscious was the ultimate causative factor in their arrest.

Perhaps further light can be shed on this point. Remember the example when, after a period of abstinence from smoking, the husband reached for his wife's burning cigarette in the ashtray and smoked it? This was a subconscious act because he admitted he was at a loss to understand why he did it.

That's equally true of persons who get themselves arrested. Oftentimes they'll admit they do not know why their reactions were not different. "If only I had not reacted like I did then I would not have been arrested," they complain. Certainly they would not consciously approach a police officer and say "Please arrest me because I have just committed a crime"? However, by their actions and behavior they, in effect, say the same thing!

I remember when this conclusion first became rooted in my mind. It was at the Texas Department of Corrections (now called the Texas Criminal Justice System). I attended an Alcoholics Anonymous meeting there and, after learning I had written a book, *"Crack, You and Your Love Ones"*, I was invited to speak to a group of inmates. I had just begun to appreciate the role of the subconscious mind as the seat of all our habits.

It was pointed out to my audience that no one consciously intended to be in prison. There was no conscious effort to be there. On the contrary, if the results of our actions had been foreseen we most certainly would have reacted differently. But just as the impulsive taking of the cigarette by the husband from the ashtray was outside his conscious will just so were the actions that led to being arrested outside the conscious will of the inmates. In each case they were determined by that "force" within us that governs behavior, our subconscious minds.

The response to my address was unexpected and overwhelmingly favorable. I instantly became a virtual celebrity among the inmates. Everywhere I went someone would invariably approach me with praise and congratulations. Something I sensed in all of them motivated me to intensify my effort to share this knowledge. I sensed that they not only needed this information but they really *wanted* it. They seemed to realize that by means of knowing the role of the subconscious they could now somehow better help themselves. They were persistent in their questions as to how to proceed. What practical steps could be taken by them to reprogram their subconscious minds? I had many of them come to me later and say they had begun daily meditations and verbal affirmations and that they really were beginning to feel good about themselves. They knew their recovery had begun.

As the meetings continued the inmates cast aside their reservations and began to share their experiences. The "God of your understanding" concept was easily embraced by all (even Atheists) and an atmosphere of spirituality began to be felt by all. In fact the spiritual principles of love, humility, sharing, acceptance and honesty permeated the meetings and seemed to replace the old attitudes of selfishness, denial, arrogance and resentment that are the unfailing signs of addiction.

What was really taking place was something of which I was not aware. At that time I knew only results were being obtained. All who attended the meetings were not only clean but, in addition, they were serene. The controlled environment virtually assured them there would be no drug usage (although drugs do find their way into prisons). More important however, was the serenity that existed. The good feeling of knowing you are at peace with yourself and those of the fellowship. This is the essential ingredient that must be present in the mixture if the danger of relapse is to be avoided. Without being serene, as earlier pointed out, one can be as mentally distraught as the alcoholic in need of a drink.

At any rate, what I was not aware of was just how the change I saw was taking place. I knew how, on an individual basis and by means of verbal affirmations the subconscious is reprogrammed but did not fully understand it.

What I did not know nor understand was how it was accomplished on a much larger scale.

I was unaware that the programming of the subconscious by conscious selection of thoughts on the one hand could be equated with the conscious exposure to experiences and practices on the other. Actually the only difference was that one involved individual mediation while the other concerned itself with group participation.

Perhaps I should not say that I didn't know how change and development takes place. Rather that I was not aware at the time of how to apply it to the process of addictions in general. That is a much more accurate statement.

With this application of the universal laws of change and in particular that of transformation of quantity into quality, it became possible to correctly articulate the coming into being, growth into development plus the ultimate passing away of our addictions.

I do not intend to belabor the point as to the importance of this law but if it is to have the desired impact on the demand for drugs, it is crucial that it be thoroughly understood. This means each and every individual addict desiring to become and stay clean, be able to apply it in his daily life.

With regard to the first attempt to explain the law, it was said that "a certain amount of something applied to something, at a definite point in time gives rise to something else." Further, *that* "something else" is always different and usually opposite of "what was before." This is a relatively simple way of saying that "quantitative changes at some point always produce results that are quite different and very noticeable." In other words if we were to observe a certain process or thing during its quantitative stages of change and then observe it after it has changed qualitatively (at a certain point in time) not only would it be "noticeable" but it would be entirely different and perhaps even the opposite of what it was before the changes took place.

Let's take an example: We observe the second hand move as the clock steadily ticks the seconds away. Each tick is a gradual and continuous quantitative change. The minute hand movement is not noticeable. The quantitative movement of the minute hand merely reflects the change taking place in our universe as the day proceeds. Although these changes are gradual, imperceptive, and not noticeable yet at a certain point during the day a qualitative change in form comes into existence. The changes then become noticeable. They are also different. Day changes into night. Not only is night different from day but it is the exact opposite. If we were to observe things at night they would be entirely different than they would be if observed during the day.

Now we will use an example as it applies to addiction: "A" is addicted to crack cocaine but he has a strong commitment to turn his life around. He understands the root of his problem lies in his subconscious mind and that it's necessary to reprogram it in order for recovery to be successful. He regularly involves himself in meditation and verbal affirmations at night before retiring for bed. He does this consciously and consistently (quantitatively). Moreover he attends a group treatment program regularly. He meets new people, cultivates new relationships and develops new interests. He mentions to his girlfriend, from whom he is separated, that he is in recovery. She doesn't believe what he says since the changes aren't noticeable (they are gradual and imperceptible). Furthermore, she's been misled by him before.

After a while (approximately one month) she sees him in person. She immediately notices the change. His attitude is different. His appearance is different. Whereas before he was arrogant and resentful, now he radiates acceptance and humility. He does not appear to be the same person. New interest in him is rekindled because he has virtually changed into his opposite.

In both of these examples we can see that the quantitative changes are the *cause* and the qualitative change, the *effect*.

It can be seen then, why we should be aware of, and direct our efforts to, the quantitative aspects of change, this we must do if we want to determine and influence the development of any phenomenon, process or thing. If we desire to change *what is into what it can become*, we can do it.

We know from our understanding of the universal law of change and development that things are not separate, categorized and unchanging, that the either *this* or *that* classification is not in accord with how things really are. We know that something can be *what it is* and at the same time be that *which it is becoming*.

What is becoming is determined by the nature of the quantitative pressures, changes and experiences to which any given process or thing is subjected.

It is precisely here that we can, by means of our "conscious selection" and "will", determine and influence the direction and character of what is becoming.

By choosing to regularly meditate and plant positive non drug oriented seeds in our subconscious garden, in addition to exposing it to non drug oriented experiences and relationships, we change ourselves from addicts to non addicts.

Of course if we did none of these things we would still change because, as we have learned, nothing permanently impedes change. If we did not make the above choice the result would be a change in the opposite direction. A negative direction resulting in the deepening of our addiction. Remember what we said about the status quo?

Remember also that this was proven when Albert Einstein showed that the atoms existing throughout the universe were in a constant state of motion. What appeared to be motionless was merely where the atoms moved so slowly as to appear to be not moving at all! The example given was the growth process of our fingernails.

It's important to determine whether or not you *truly* want to change *what is into what can be*, notice I said *can be*.

I say this because even though a process or state of existence can become something else other that what it is yet does not necessarily follow that it will become what we *want* it to be. It may become what we *don't want* it to be. This is extremely likely and almost a certainty if we do nothing and thus allow the same negative thoughts and experiences that cause our wretched condition of addiction, in the first place to prevail.

This is when the positive and negative aspects of quantitative change assume primary importance. They are the keys to staying clean. They are the most significant and the most susceptible to our conscious control.

It is precisely because we can choose the seeds to plant in our subconscious garden; it is precisely because we *can* choose the thoughts, and experiences and relationships we desire to take root there. It is for these reasons that the positive aspect of the quantitative process alone holds the key to our recovery.

If we accentuate the positive and eliminate the negative, we will recover.

The universal laws discussed then, are nothing less than the "rules of the game." The main objective is for the addict to "play by them."

Now more than ever habits can be overcome on a scale greater than ever before because a scientific method is within the reach of all who truly want it. For those who, for various reasons, are reluctant to submit to professional group treatment there is an alternative, especially in the initial stage of recovery. They can be on their own, undertake the same basic procedure used by the most successful programs.

Essential to doing this is being able to think in terms of movement and change; in terms of things and processes forever coming into existence, growing, developing and the passing away; the old being replaced by the new ad infinitum. In this way we can effectively begin to recover from our addiction but it is not recommended beyond the initial stage.

The main reason for this is that although as individuals we may be able to refrain from using and remain clean for extended periods of time, yet we will probably not be serene. We will not have peace of mind, we are still aware of a frightening illness that lingers inside of us. This awareness can and often does reflect itself in many emotionally unhealthy forms. Feelings of paranoia, anorexia, guilt, worry and denial becomes our constant companions often competing for space in our consciousness. This is so because of the social void that has been created by our attacking the problem on our own. After all, man is a social animal and the principle advantage of group therapy is recognition of this fact. We can talk about our feelings with others who have had similar experiences. We can apply the experiences of others to our own situation and thus see if there are lessons to be learned, inevitably we will meet people with long periods of clean time, some of whose experiences will parallel ours. Direct benefit results. When we see, through social interaction, just how much there is to be gained, we begin to embrace one of the most fundamental spiritual principles needed for successful recovery. This is humility, and it logically flows from sharing the knowledge of specific problems with others. It is the height of spiritual growth.

Applying the ideas and principles of those with clean time to our own problems produces positive changes within us. This is the main advantage of group therapy. By attending the meetings we supplement what we are able to do on our own. We realize that sharing is a powerful weapon. We seek a person who has been clean for quite some time and with his or her help are able to gain invaluable feedback. It is an undeniable fact that no one can help a recovering addict as much as another addict who is also in recovery.

Staying clean then becomes a joy. Serenity peaks. We are now on our way to, not a short-lived, but sustained and solid recovery. We are now on our way because we are becoming totally transformed spiritually into our opposite. There is no further need to attempt persuasion of those still suffering by mere words alone.

We become a shining example of the beacon of hope. Armed with the correct philosophical outlook of the process of change, we can delight in our awareness of what's happening in our subconscious mind. We are joyously aware of the multitude of "seeds" daily bombarding it and taking root in its garden. They are positive seeds. They are environmental seeds. They are the seeds of our newly formed relationships.

As previously noted both individual meditation with verbal affirmations and group treatment experiences reach the subconscious essentially the same way.

There must be feelings of faith and conviction accompanying them before they descend into the subconscious garden. For instance when indulging in verbal affirmations you must literally "see" yourself becoming the person you want to be. You should speak with conviction. Remember you shouldn't say "I *want* to become drug free" but rather "*I am becoming drug free!*"

Once the results of meditation and verbal affirmations are experienced and appreciated by the individual, he will then begin to understand and appreciate the broader scope of professional group therapy. By means of these established programs the rate of progress will increase and more importantly the likelihood of relapse will be virtually eliminated. It will be realized that the subconscious, like a sponge, can soak up the multitude of experiences given to it by the group programs just as easily as it can accept the seeds planted by solitary meditation. The reprogramming process is the same in both cases. Furthermore, it is even more effective if the individual and group programs are combined. Such combinations insure the most rapid transformation possible from an addictive to a non addictive existence.

Above all the bottom line prerequisite is not the need but the desire to quit. The addict must truly *want* to quit, not merely *think* they want to stop. However, the overwhelming majority of those I've met who are suffering from the agony of addiction are not happy with their situation.

If the American people were privy to a national poll where addicts respond to the question "Would you prefer being free from addiction or are you satisfied with your present condition?" I am certain they would be surprised.

I can, personally, recall only the one addict who seemingly and forthrightly declared satisfaction with her addiction. I say "seemingly" because I truly believe even she was being dishonest and merely trying to hide behind a façade of contentment. Happy addicts are virtually non existent. Their mind-set blocks out their pleasurable pre-addictive experiences. If this were not so I believe they would more readily enter treatment programs.

The Subconscious-Physiological Basis

In retrospect, the origin of this book dates back to my daughter's pre-med studies at Stanford. As my son and I listened attentively, she gave a lucid account of conception and the process from fertilization of the female ovum to actual delivery at birth.

I talked with her by phone and recalled the lecture given by her to Craig and me. I told her I intended to use it as an analogy to demonstrate the universal laws of change and development. During our conversation she imparted another gem of information to me which actually reinforced my conviction that I was on the right tract as far as my thesis was concerned.

She told me that during the initial period of cell division, within the uterus, a group of highly specialized cells separate into sort of a plateau. This, she said, is the first and hence, most fundamental cell specialization leading to organ development.

After separation of these cells there takes place a folding under, convolution, if you will, into what is called the "neural tube." This "neural tube" is the forerunner of the central and autonomic nervous systems as well as the brain.

We previously were shown that environmental circumstances invariably influence the development of every process or form of existence. We saw in both examples of the incubated egg and the male and female relationship that external circumstances (quantitatively) inevitably change "something" into "something else." What's more we now know this "something else" is oftentimes the "opposite" of what was before.

So it was with my relapse. From a state of non addiction which resulted from positive drug free environmental influences, I was again in a state of addiction because of negative drug oriented circumstances; the exact opposite of what was before.

Environmental conditions are the external circumstances that always determine the course of development and change which occurs within every process and form of existence.

As we have seen the decisive factor is our "conscious selection." By means of it we have the power to determine the direction we desire our development to proceed. This is the secret that one suffering from addiction must sense and utilize if he is to be successful in redirecting his life. It is this way that one can control one's own destiny!

It must be kept in mind that change is inevitable. It must also be remembered that there is internal as well as external change.

Internal change and development has a dynamic of its own. We can do nothing about it. That "which is" is also becoming "something else" whether we like it or not. External circumstances play an active role in assuring this. However, what something can or cannot become is determined by its "internal content."

Environment and Lifestyle

Another M.D., in addition to my daughter, furnished me with important material in support of my thesis. He is Dr. Ira J. Chasnoff, president of the National Association for Prenatal Addiction Research and Education. Dr. Chasnoff is an expert in prenatal addiction. He spoke to a group of health care professionals at Scott & White Memorial Hospital in Temple, Texas. His topic was "how mother's habits affect the unborn child."

"The single most common cause of diagnosable mental retardation in the United States is fetal alcohol syndrome," he said, "it's related to the mother's drinking during pregnancy." He said children born to mother's who used drugs such as crack cocaine can suffer even missing limbs. This could result even if the mother used it only once or twice.

"Tobacco is responsible for low birth weight," he emphasized, "and if a baby is born weighing less than (5 lbs. 8 ozs.) there is a 30 times more likelihood of dying the first year of life. It is the leading cause of death among infants."

He said, "It's time, and past time, for lawmakers, employers, health care providers, and consumers to be educated about the critical link between health, nutrition, *behavior*, lifestyle, education and *environmental conditions.*"

I couldn't agree with him more. As far as successfully dealing with addiction one desperately needs "to be educated about the critical link between behavior, lifestyle and environmental conditions." In fact that, in essence is the main thrust of this book.

It was precisely because of not being educated as to the "critical link between behavior and environmental conditions" that I relapsed. Perhaps I knew there was a connection but underestimated it. In my mind I was going to change the environment. Of course this can be done but not the extent that *we* can be changed by our *environment*.

When I visited my old "friends" in the hope to persuade them to become clean like me, I downplayed the critical link between the external environmental circumstances and me.

Instead of developing new relations, new interest and frequenting new places of a positive nature, I chose the opposite. I resumed exposing myself to the same environmental influences that had given rise to and perpetuated my addiction.

We previously were shown that environmental circumstances invariably influence the development of every process of form of existence. We saw in both examples of the incubated egg and the male and female relationship that external circumstances (quantitatively) inevitably change "something" into "something else." What's more we now know this "something else" is oftentimes the "opposite" of what was before.

So it was with my relapse. From a state of non addiction which resulted from positive drug free environmental influences, I was again in a state of addiction because of negative drug oriented circumstances; the exact opposite of what was before.

Environmental conditions are the external circumstances that *always* determine the course of development and change which occurs within every process and form of existence.

As we have seen the decisive factor is our "conscious selection." By means of it we have the power to determine the direction we desire our development to proceed. This is the secret that one suffering from addiction must sense and utilize if he is to be successful in redirecting his life. It is this way that he can control his own destiny!

It must be kept in mind that change is inevitable. It must also be remembered that there is internal as well as external change.

Internal change and development has dynamism of its own. We can do nothing about it. That "which is" is also becoming "something else" whether we like it or not. External circumstances play an active role in assuring this. However, what something can or cannot become is determined by its "internal content."

The egg has an internal content of its own. No amount of external influence can change it into anything but a chicken. Of course, assuming it's a chicken egg.

We have an internal dynamic of our own. We are either addicts becoming non addicts or addicts becoming more entrenched addicts.

There is no status quo. Positive or negative environmental influences are the keys. Our "conscious selection" is the determining factor.

We alone hold the power, through it, to use these keys. In the final analysis we are the ones who determine our own destiny!

CB Warsteane, J.D.

End

Epilogue

The road to recovery from addiction presented here will, inevitably, lead to an addiction-free life. I have traveled it.

My prison experience has been instrumental in validating this conviction. The prison process, like all processes, is subject to the universal laws of change and development. It too, has its contradiction, its unity of opposites, its positive as well as its negative aspects.

If the positive is "accentuated" and the negative "minimized", the inescapable conclusion is that rather than merely getting arrested, I was in fact "rescued!" Therefore, instead of harboring bitterness and resentment, I am truly gratified to the Texas Justice System for providing the positive circumstances by means of which I was able to completely reprogram my subconscious mind. It is my firm conviction that, had I not been incarcerated, a worse fate would have befallen me; it would have been death.

I am grateful for what I have received and realize that it "can only be kept by giving it away." It is in the spirit of it being "more blessed to give than to receive" that the proven method for overcoming addictions was presented here; for, indeed, we *all* have them.

The people of drug producing countries have a powerfully valid response to United States' criticism of the exportation of drugs to America, they argue that if the demand for cocaine and heroin wasn't so great in the United States there would be no basis for wholesale drug trafficking to flourish.

They are right, while it's important to interdict the flow of drugs into the nation yet it is not the supply that must be targeted but the demand. Once the demand for the poison is drastically reduced the profits will dwindle and drug dealers will go out of business. If there is no profitable market it will make no economic sense to continue production.

However that would require a different course of action than the one presently being pursued by the policy makers of our nation.

It would necessitate placing the political emphasis on rehabilitation. Now it is on incarceration which, unfortunately, regards addiction to illegal drugs as a crime rather than an illness.

A significant reason for this is economics. The flourishing prison industrial complex derives huge profits from an abundant supply of unpaid prison labor. But the drug war will never be won until the demand is diminished.

It is with that purpose foremost in mind, together with the happiness to be achieved by overcoming one's addiction, that this book was written.

C B W